Hot Summer Nights 2014

a collection of Erotic Poetry, Prose & Stories

inner child press, ltd.

my lusts are taking advantage of my weaknesses....

and i am beginning to forget who i thought i was....

General Information

Hot Summer Nights 2014
a collection of Erotic Poetry, Prose & Stories
Anthology

1st Edition : 2014

This Publishing is protected under Copyright Law as a "Collection". All rights for all submissions are retained by the Individual Author and or Artist. No part of this Publishing may be Reproduced, Transferred in any manner without the prior **WRITTEN CONSENT** of the "Material Owner" or it's Representative Inner Child Press. Any such violation infringes upon the Creative and Intellectual Property of the Owner pursuant to International and Federal Copyright Law. Any queries pertaining to this "Collection" should be addressed to Publisher of Record.

Publisher Information
1st Edition : Inner Child Press
innerchildpress@gmail.com
www.innerchildpress.com

This Collection is protected under U.S. and International Copyright Laws

Copyright © 2014 : The Erotic Poets & Writers

ISBN-13 : 978-0692244654 (Inner Child Press, Ltd.)
ISBN-10 : 0692244654

$ 19.95 : B & W

Cover Graphics : Chyna Blue
Edifyin' Graphix
edifyin.graphix@gmail.com

> *"An orgasm a day keeps the doctor away"*
>
> Mae West

Dedication

This collection is dedicated

to all the people

upon this Beautiful Planet

who choose to embrace their Passions.

All for Love.

we have laid down the expressions
of our desires and our wantonness
upon the sheets within

peel back the covers
and take a journey with us
as we explore each others erotica
come . . . .

~ 'just bill'

Preface

Well . . . here we go again, another episode where the writers have "come" together to express their desires, fantasies and experiences pertaining Erotica.

There are many souls about us who are still yet uncomfortable with their lusts and dreams about such things. We will pray for them . . . some day. In the mean time we are busy attempting to discover our deepest self by peeling back the *"sheets"* of pretense that Society says are acceptable. After all, this is the 21st century is it not? The dark ages were a long time ago . . . for some, but still exists for many in the form of Indoctrinations and other Taboos.

Erotica skirts somewhere between our Passions, Sensuality and all out . . . well . . . let's call it Porn for now. But as we truthfully know, many of us do have pornographic thoughts . . . yes ? This offering is not about bringing those type of words to you, for that can be acquired anywhere on the internet. No, what we are attempting to do is couple our creative writing gifts and talents with our Verse, Prose and Short Story to provide you with an inspiring reading companion during those Hot Summer Nights of 2014 . . . . enjoy.

Blessed Be

Bill

"Now piercèd is her virgin zone;
She feels the foe within it.
She hears a broken amorous groan,
The panting lover's fainting moan,
Just in the happy minute."

John Wilmot
The Complete Poems

Table of Contents

Dedication — v
Preface — vii

The Writes

Kimberly Burnham	1
Alicia C. Cooper	3
Tony Henninger	5
Charles 'Seabe' Banks & Starr Poetress	6
Iram Fatima 'Ashi'	10
Kerstin Centervall	22
Gracey Flynn	23
Alan W. Jankowski	24
David W. Landrumn	43
Alesha Aris	64
James Moore	65
Janet Renee Cryer	66
Elizabeth Jones	69
santiba, aka Su(e)NiaDiyg	72
Ann Betz	73
Ann White	74
Mr O. and Gracey Flyn	75

Table of Content ... continued

Anthony Modungwo	76
Neville Hiatt	78
Matt Parker	79
Flowetic Justice	81
Justice Clarke	86
C. William Clarke	89
Mellenne Carpenter	96
Jaz Gill	97
Dr. Kiriti Sengupta	99
Ananya Chatterjee	100
Laura Lee Sugah	101
Laura Lee Sweet	102
Jason Constantine Ford	107
Gail Weston Shazor	108
Meghna Gupta Jogani	110
Jamie Bond	118
Janet P. Caldwell	120
William S. Peters, Sr.	121

Epilogue 133

other Anthologies	135

it's beginning to get a little hot in here . . .

don't you think?

Lust and Love have no barriers....

Hot Summer Nights 2014

a collection of Erotic Poetry, Prose & Stories

inner child press, ltd.

all i know is that i want you . . . .

The Erotic Poets & Writers

Winking Across The Campground

Only a little intimidated,
I winked
at her across the rocky campground
after all
full of a knight's adrenaline
on an expedition
bicycling 3000 miles
across the US
Knowing she rides
only the first week
a wink seems harmless
telling myself
I am not really flirting.
in the realm of newness
a little off balance
It changes you,
the challenge
riding 70 miles a day,
waking up inside
new places every morning,
beside her for a week
feeling sunlight
the wind sometimes
blowing straight in your face
stealing your breath
the sounds of green
at your side
interrupted by the boom
of zoom zoom
It's hard
to get your bearings
the push pull
you are always moving

Hot Summer Nights 2014

towards the horizon
the fiery sun setting on a life
away from her
away from the known
towards the unknowable
And sometimes you do
that magically unpredictable thing
that turns out amazing
so now joined
our hearts journey
steady in different ways
to be together.

Kimberly Burnham, PhD,

Inner Child Press Poetry Posse
www.amazon.com/Kimberly-Burnham/e/B0054RZ4A0

Sashay

His mahogany gaze

Follows my sashay

Bounces with my bounce

Sways with my sway

And I am tempted to be coy

And veil my undress

Drape my shoulders in black silk

Slip lace cups over my breasts

But I don't

'Cause I can't;

He has stolen my care

Tossed my no's into the fire

And my maybe's into the air

And stained these once vanilla walls

With fifty shades of red

Created hot rhythms as we sweated the sheets

To the beat from the springs of the bed

He has drank white wine from my womanly wells

Licked sweetness from the line of my lips

His fingers have traced the length of my pearl

Played house in the hub of my hips

Hot Summer Nights 2014

Thus hiding would be quite silly now

And I permit him to have his fill

The flames that flash in the pools of his eyes

Make me melt so I bend to his will

So, tonight as his mahogany gaze

Follows my sashay

His fixation on my frame

No longer daunts

Because nothing quite compares

To the sight of a master

Who's just been bested by

The very one he taught

Alicia C. Cooper

http://www.innerchildpress.com/alicia-c-cooper.php

The Erotic Poets & Writers

YEAH BABE, THAT'S IT…

Making my way along
your delicious inner thighs,
traveling a serpentine path.
Getting closer to the prize.
The gates of heaven are waiting
to open for me, only me.
I begin to taste the rose attar,
as a fine dew forms slowly,
relishing every drop I inhale.
Ahhh, the sweet aroma of you.
Looking up into your eyes
my soul bursts into flame.
So lost, I can't remember who
I am, or whence I came.
You take me in and, both,
let me go and hold me tight.
Speed up. Slow down. Yeah, babe,
that's it. That's just right.
In this ecstatic rhythm we remain.
Our hearts beating a faster pace.
Passing the point of no return.
Tighter and tighter our embrace.
Falling through the skies.
Landing in paradise.
Not wanting this dream to wane,
we start it all again and again.
Yeah, babe, that's it.
That's just right. Mmmm…

Tony Henninger

http://www.innerchildpress.com/tony-henninger.php

Hot Summer Nights 2014

Zero Sum Fucks

seaBe

Three Fuckly wuckie
Two Fuckly wuckie
One Fuckly wuckie
Zero Fucks
Whether U the Door or the one going thru
Sum of all fucks=
Zero
Memory left to you
Slamming the door
Sum = same
same Positions
Matters not..
In fucked
Out unfucked
Zero some /sums Fucks
Could I
Zero cums Fucks
I wish I
Can I take it back to Zero

starr

Ha, You wished you got three Fuckly Wuckies from me,
I remembered as you pleading on your knees,
All the times you ever tried,
You always wanted it from the backside,
So as you try to erase me,
Remember no more Fuckly Wuckie from me,
Your hand will have to be your new she

No more sitting on my knees or bending over as you please,
No more being the first the drink your juice,
So while you are wishing she was loose,
Remember who could wrap her legs around your neck ,
Now you remember, that's right who puts who in check
Zero Sum Fucks

seaBe

She shiTts me ...Gets away never… misses from me....ever wish we never met...Confuses me...taken a back the Fucks we Had...

starr

I am betting you still like it in the corner,

seaBe

all your corners are a delight.!

starr

Ha, that was so long ago, I bet I was never an after thought,
I was just a fuck for the passing of time
how you like to poke in the butt as you have me bending over the balcony for everyone to see

seaBe

wild hair flying....sweat grinding ...for everyone to see..!!

Hot Summer Nights 2014

starr

Ahh those were the times if I hadn't been more than a fuck
to you as you had me believing it was
real

seaBe

dream state...believing I've met my ...mate...the world looks
small .. when I'm inside her!!.. so
real...!!!

starr

The juicy, wet, flesh will make any man think it is real but
when we are not laying, you mind
wonders as I am not on it unless you are in it

seaBe

wondering if she'll give me sum.....the big dinner she ate
like a Coalminers son...filling up like I
want to feel her Hum...only our first date....

starr

Forced that that $2 meal down my throat, we'd been better
off going to taco bell than his home...
where's the beef?
I don't know what do you think...
Even though he was a zero sum fuck,
He knew how to work it in pain free,
When the night is cold and the bed I'm tucked,
He will be the one I remember that fuck pleasured me...

seaBe

not...a Fuck of ...but a Zero sum fuck of...
She wasn't Bad..especially on the stairs...
but am I Glad .....just a liTTle... that she's gone...
sum nites I long for her....but I'm stronger with out her...

I'm better without her...she tried to strangle a Brother...
kiSSes and Loves wasn't good enough for her
She wanted more...!
Zero love sum...Gone.....

staRR/seaBe

http://www.amazon.com/Janet-Renee-Cryer/e/B00BED5CEQ

http://www.innerchildpress.com/charles-seabe-banks.php

Hot Summer Nights 2014

Drowning Out

I drown into a deep, bottomless ocean

Into the dark depths of the unknown, through the seas of agony!

Going though the bay, I feel cold and lifeless,

Pain has numbed my body, there's no soul left inside of me!

How I had waited for you, my soul mate

But then the moment of separation, slashed me into two!

I screamed silently, and slept for centuries,

To forgive and forget you, Alas! Pain would not letting me die!

Iram Fatima 'Ashi'

The Compromise

It would have been just another of those dark calm nights of my life, if not for the sandstorm. I was on night duty and the streets bore a deserted look. The visibility was low, and my watch glimmered with 03:00. I was just done seeing my patients and had just entered my cabin. I felt a little tired and dull and couldn't help but yawn. I kept my stethoscope on the table and sat on my chair trying to relax. I looked out of the window for a while; I knew it was going to be a long, long night. I opened the half-read novel which was lying in the drawers for weeks now.

When I was about to read, nurse Suzan came to report an emergency and that I had to be there ASAP. 'What a great night' I thought to myself. I placed the book back to where it belonged, picked up my stethoscope and ran towards the emergency ward.

There was a young girl lying unconsciousness on a stretcher. I ordered to shift her on bed number six in the emergency ward. 'What happened to her?' I asked the bearded man, whom I assumed to be her father. He looked like he was in his fifties and was standing alongside the patient.

'She had food poisoning.' He replied nervously. I could smell the lie in his words. 'Sir, if you want to see your girl make through this. You will have to tell me the truth.' I had an idea about what he was holding back. 'She consumed her mother's sleeping pills.' He said with a grim face.

I rushed to provide her medical care. I had an oxygen pipe fixed on one of her nasals and a cannula inside another nasal for gastric lavage to drain toxic from inside. There was another cannula on her right wrist for the supply of Saline water. It wasn't a good sight. She looked to be in her twenties. She must have acted on impulse, like most of the pampered children these days do. I instructed a nurse to monitor her condition and came out of the room.

When I looked at the faces of her parents, I felt like going back and giving her a tight slap. Right then, I had no sympathy for her pale face, dried lips and lean body. Her parents had done nothing wrong to deserve this! People like these are habitual of having all their demands fulfilled and when things don't go according to their plan, they lose their balance and commit such stupidity. They should for once, think of what they are putting their parents through!

My mind was in a state of anger, part of me wanted to go to her father and console him but I went straight to my cabin to get out of the emotional web. I opened the book again, to get it all off my head, but soon the nurse came back running to me, 'Doctor, her pulse rate is slowing down and so is her blood pressure!' I again rushed towards the ward. I noticed her breathing problem. I gave her a few injections and kept sitting near her bed until her condition was stable.

I ran a quick glance at her face; she was glowing with calmness as if her soul was ready to fly away. I realized we were struggling to save a girl who didn't want to be saved; she was looking forward to find peace in the afterlife. It seemed as if we were fighting for a lost cause. It was my first major case since I was done with studying medicine, and I wasn't going to yield easily even if the patient had given up. I consulted some of my seniors and read a few books on such cases.

After completing my shift I came back to my place, but her thoughts had followed me all the way home. This had happened for the first time that a patient had made such a serious impact on me. My mother couldn't help but notice my disturbed state. She said with a smile, 'I see a preoccupied doctor has taken place of my son.' I ate silently and went to bed. That was the first time in my life that I experienced insomnia.

The next evening, as my shift began, I went straight to her bed. Her mother was sitting beside her. She looked at me with eyes full of hope. 'Please tell me she'd be fine. Will I be able to see her smile again?' That was a million dollar question, I had no answer for. 'She needs your prayers for now.' I said trying to keep my tone steady. I could see her eye lashes bathing in tears after listening to my answer.

'If you don't mind, can I ask you something personal?' I asked her while handing over a tissue. 'You can trust me; I will keep it to myself.' 'Sure doctor, anything. Her life is in your hands.' she wiped the tears off her eyes. 'Why did she do this to herself?' She paused for a moment, and then spoke, 'My daughter loved a boy very much. And he got married to someone else, yesterday. She just couldn't accept that.'

'Oh! Does he know about this?' I asked. 'No, we just shifted to this city some three-four months back and she was sure that the boy would come asking for her hand. They were good friends. But she loved him very much and thought he loved him back but he married the girl of her parents' choice. 'Why didn't you try contacting him?' The questions in my mind were endless.

'We were not aware of the depth of her emotions for him until we read the note she left last night' her eyes were going wet again. For the first time in my life, I could feel someone else's pain as if it were my own. Her foolishness was just a consequence of her innocence. She was like a little kid who needed looking after. This case had become very personal now.

It was the fourth night now; my thoughts were all focused on that bed where she lay. My shift was over; it was really late at night. I went to check on her one last time before leaving. I noticed she was restless, still unconscious. It seemed to me as if she wanted to say something, but didn't have the words to express. I looked around; there was no one else in the room but me. I gently touched her forehead, it was a little warm. I caressed her hair trying to relax her.

There were a lot of things that I wanted to tell her. I wanted her to know that it will all be alright soon. I wanted her to feel my presence, that I had got her back now. And I wasn't going to rest until I had fixed everything. I gently kissed her forehead and took her hand, placing it on my heart. 'See, I feel your pain too'.

She whispered something back in her sleep. Was it 'stay' or was it 'never leave me'? I guess I can never be sure. I remember being by her side for hours until it was morning and I heard footsteps approaching; I wiped the tears off my eyes. It was the nurse, she gave her some painkillers. After sometime she was calm again.

After spending those moments with her, who to me was better than an eternity, I could feel that I wasn't the same person anymore. I had changed, now my world revolved around her. I had only one purpose in my life now, to save her. I gave her more attention than I ever gave to any of my patients. It was only after that day, that she started showing signs of improvement. She even gained consciousness. Everyone at the hospital called it a miracle.

It was the seventh day now; I reached hospital before time as if driven by some divine force. Senior Doctor Arvind called me to make all the discharge papers ready for Alia. She was now good enough to be released. I was happy for her, but part of me was finding it hard to believe that she wouldn't be around anymore.

Hot Summer Nights 2014

I rushed towards her bed; she was staring at the walls of hospital as if trying to find herself. Her face was still a bit pale and her eyes were showing her inner hollowness, but she looked way better today. 'How are you feeling now, Alia?' I asked her. She looked at me with annoyance, which really stung. How I had hoped she'd remember what happened that night between us and greet me with a smile. But contrary to my expectations, I was just like any other stranger. My presence was more of an intrusion to her. She went back to staring at the wall.

Her mother finally filled the dead-air, 'She's better now, thanks to your efforts doctor.' She then introduced me to her, 'Alia this is Dr. Danish Ali, if not for him, you wouldn't be alive today.' I noticed a frown on her face when she heard the last words from her mother's mouth, as if I had done something really bad bringing her back to life. Her eyes were still fixed on the wall. It was all too much for me to take. I struggled to let out a smile, everything had now gone blur.

'She's good to go now. But she'll have to make regular visits to the hospital. Dr. Sharma will be taking charge of the counseling. He's the best psychiatric that we've got.' I handed over the discharge papers to her parents and she was released from my care.

Her absence was something really hard to get used-to with. But somehow I had managed to get past a week, thanks to the sleeping pills. It was just another day at the office when

I was working on an afternoon shift. I was walking through the corridor when my eyes met hers again. I didn't want to stop and say hello, but it wasn't like I had a choice. Her father nodded in gratitude.

'So how are you doing now Alia?' I said. 'Good.' She said, trying her best to smile. I continued my stroll after sensing the awkwardness. As I moved on, I realized her beautiful face, her sparkling eyes, and her deep enchanting dimples were all I wanted in life. I knew I had fallen in love.

When I told my mother that I'd finally decided on getting married, I swear she was the happiest person on earth. And then I told her who the girl was, and the circumstances in which we'd met. She thought I had gone completely insane. For days she tried to persuade me that I had mistaken 'sympathy' for 'love' and it was just an infatuation; that I was mixing my professional life with my personal life.

When my father came to know about it, even he couldn't find any sense in getting his son married to a girl with suicidal tendencies. 'What if she never loves you back, son?' He tried his best too, but I was really adamant. 'It's either Alia or no one.' I gave them my ultimatum. And finally they had to give in against my new found obstinacy.

So one fine Sunday morning we went to Alia's home unannounced. Our visit came as a big surprise to them, and when we explained the purpose of our visit, they didn't really know how to react. Her mother asked me to tell her

Hot Summer Nights 2014

the news myself, since they were really scared to do it themselves. 'She's been through a lot lately. And in the end, it's her decision who she wants to spend her life with.' said the father.

I was on my way to her room; I could hear someone playing a melancholic tune on a piano. It was sad but mesmerizing, I just stood right outside her room. Waiting for her to finish and then knocked her door. She opened it, stunned to see me. 'Your father sent me here; I got something to talk about.' I said trying to sound confident.

She let me in, there was a sofa lying in the corner. I sat on it, I don't remember being so nervous ever before in my life. I looked around; the walls had amazing sketches and paintings. 'So you are a painter too.' I said with a smile.

She paused for a moment and then spoke, 'Look Mr. Danish, I really appreciate everything you've done for me and with all due respect you got paid for your care. I don't think I can marry you.' Her tone was harsh and hurting. 'How do you know for sure that I'm here to ask you for marriage?' She had caught me off guard. 'Then why else would you be here? I've told pa that I don't want to marry anyone, why doesn't he ever give up?' She looked angry and hurt, but this was my only chance.

'Look, it's not him, it's me. I fell in love with you, the very first time I saw you. I just didn't realize it until you were gone. I know it might be hard for you to believe, but I have never felt so strongly for someone. Yes, I want to marry you, because I love you.' I opened my heart without a second thought.

'I don't need your sympathy Mr. Danish and I have no love left to give. I think it will be best if you leave now.' She was as cold as snow on arctic would be; I didn't have anything else to say. I stood up and left.

That was a long, long drive back home. I didn't tell anything to my mom and dad about my conversation with Alia. But they had an idea. Days turned into weeks and weeks turned into months and months into a year. I knew she was never going to say 'yes' to my proposal. But every now and then I'd torture myself with hope that may be she'll remember what had happened that night in the hospital my tender emotions, my honest love and selfless care and come running to me, which never happened.

One day I was back home late after work, my mom called me saying she'd something to talk about. I knew it would be about marrying a girl of her choice. My mother was sitting with photographs of a girl. She said, 'Son, your father and I have chosen a girl for you. We are sure you'd like her. She's…' I interrupted her. 'You know my answer. I love Alia, and I know she'd come back to me one day. It's just a matter of time.' Her insensitive attitude annoyed me.

'There comes a time when you have to move on. Everybody does that. I can't see you living like this

Hot Summer Nights 2014

anymore. I care for your happiness.' She was getting all sentimental again. 'I can't move on.' I said, starting to leave for my room. 'Perhaps you should. In fact, she has.' Her tone was sharp now. 'What do you mean?' I turned back. 'She got married last week. Her father had invited us, but we didn't tell you. We knew it would have hurt you a lot.' Her words didn't make any sense. That wasn't just possible! 'Who is the guy?' I was perplexed. 'Some U.S based engineer, she didn't even bother to meet before saying yes.' She said.

'What? How can that be?' It was all very hard to accept. 'It's true. We have been in constant touch with the family. We didn't want this to happen. But there was nothing we could have possibly done.' I wasn't ready to accept the facts; I just lost my temper 'Why didn't you tell me? I would have done something, anything! How could you do this to your own son?' That was the first time I had ever shouted at my mom. She wept and I went back to my room, trying to shut myself from the reality. I was shocked, I think the girl who was hurt in love might lose trust to believe in that emotion and may be under her family's pressure agreed to marry any unknown person and ready to accept him in her life and left her place.

I apologized to her the next day and reassured her that I'd be considering marrying the girl she'd chosen. 'I just need some time', I told her. Ten years have passed and now I am a well known surgeon in one of the private hospitals. I moved to a different city and devoted myself to the service towards mankind and only live to serve my patients. I know my parents are unhappy that I haven't got married yet. They have tried really hard, I'd give them that. Today's the day I tell my mother about the big decision that I've taken. I dialed her number, 'Hello mom! I want to marry the girl of your choice.'

I could sense the joy in her voice 'Really? So when are you coming home? I'd arrange a meeting of you two!' 'There's no need for that; I totally trust your choice. I am coming next month and you can decide any date you like.' I can sense the relief in her tone. I am just doing what Alia had done, marrying a stranger. Now I understand her idea of compromise; it doesn't really matter whether you see or meet the person you are going to marry. It will be a compromise, nevertheless. I'm just following her footsteps and there's nothing wrong in it as long as this union brings a smile upon my parents' faces.

Iram Fatima 'Ashi'

http://www.innerchildpress.com/iram-fatima-ashi.php

Hot Summer Nights 2014

Immortal Love

Make your eyes and ears to dream
Stop the time and stand completely still
You will feel the wind caressing your chin
your nose and breath almost touching the death
Don't move your arms or your hand
a snap with my fingers or a blink with my eyes
will take you to a heavenly land
cause I am the Wizard, The Witch if you want
will all my genius I make magical flaunt
I will possess you and I want to own you
and there can't be any rules for love
Your skin I will feel and your breath I will hold
until I have reached your heart and your soul
My power is not no be seen in gold
to measure my richness you must
scrutinize and behold
All my flaws are only dust
and will blow away by the lovers lust.
So keep me warm, hold my breath so close
my ghost's breath will poison your kiss
So stop the time stand completely still
I will be here for the rest of your life and if you will.

kerstin centervall

http://www.lulu.com/shop/kerstin-centervall/music-in-verses/paperback/product-21034343.html

The Erotic Poets & Writers

The Dance

Deep in the embrace of the one that I love,
in that spot where I fit like a hand in a glove.
Lost in the throes in this thing they call bliss,
entwined in the taste of a passionate kiss.
Soaring to places I've never gone before,
rising like the waves to come crashing to shore.
A flight on the wings of the one, who takes me there,
forever I could live in these moments that we share.
Purring like the lioness you searched the jungle for,
my mind tells me stop yet your sounds tell me more.
Primal these urges that now rule the day,
these moments exquisite and within them I'd stay.
Those screams are perfection as they fill up this space,
but not nearly as perfect as the look on your face.
Speaking in tongues to those that might hear,
as that moment of impact now draws so near.
A most primitive dance yet we keep in step,
on toward the never where those secrets are kept.
With a thunderous climax the whole world is gone,
a day of enlightenment and we stand at it's dawn.
The waves are now calm and the ship has stopped rocking,
upon total fulfillment our bodies can't stop knocking.

Gracey Flynn

http://www.writerscafe.org/graceyflynn

Hot Summer Nights 2014

Size Does Matter

Size does matter, if you're a car,
A bigger engine will take you real far,
Size does matter that's understood,
When we're talking about what's under the hood,
You need lots of power to make those tires squeal,
But when we're talking about women it's a whole other deal,
Because size matters when racing on a track,
But in the bedroom it's the motion in your back,
Because in a hot rod, you better have a big block,
But to a woman, it's how you use your cock,
Because in the bedroom it isn't a race,
To put that look of delight on her face,
Because in a car you need a big engine for motion,
But in romance, it's love and devotion,
So where size matters on a drag strip,
In love it's a whole other trip,
In a car it's how fast you can go,
But in the bedroom, you best take it slow,
It's no race to cross the finish line,
Take it slow and you'll do just fine,

The Erotic Poets & Writers

So remember you're a man not a car,

Do things right and you will be her star,

Because it doesn't take power and speed,

To satisfy a woman's every need,

Be honest and kind and tell her no lies,

And you'll be the man to win first prize,

Too much worry about the size of your tool,

Only makes you look like a fool,

So if you don't learn to do what you can,

She might go out and find another man,

Because size may matter for spinning your tires,

But it takes a real man to satisfy a woman's desires,

And if you can't do it she'll go out and find,

Another man who's loving and kind,

While you're all alone worrying about size,

She'll be out with some other guys,

Who may not do as well on the drag strip,

But got your woman doing a flip,

So size may help you racing on the streets,

But it ain't gonna help you between the sheets.

Alan W. Jankowski

Hot Summer Nights 2014

Dance Class

The time that I spent with Lynn, the girl I had met at the gym after my divorce, was rather blissful in many ways. Not only was she fun to be around and a great conversationalist, but she loved to try new things. This I consider a very positive attribute in a woman. Not just new restaurants and the like, but actually learning new things. Expanding our horizons, so to speak. One of the things we did together as a couple was to take ballroom dance lessons.

Prior to this time, my idea of dance was something you did at weddings after a few drinks. I am admittedly not much of a dancer. I have to say I admire those dancers you see on TV. I often envied their grace and athleticism. I sometimes imagined myself at some event, tossing my date in the air in the middle of the dance floor while everyone present looked on in wonder. Hopefully, I would be able to catch her on the way down.

Those occasional thoughts of wowing the audience on the dance floor at some relatives wedding were never enough to get me to take dance lessons. My watching competitive ballroom dancing on the television and imagining myself and a date in the spotlight seemed like something that had little or no chance of ever really happening. It ranked right up there with ultimate fighting. I sometimes imagined myself in the ring while watching the UFC, but I knew better than to ever let that happen. Until I met Lynn, I felt the same way about ballroom dancing.

Lynn somehow had remarkably persuasive powers over me. Probably something to do with the fact that she was a hot looking, athletic woman who was good in bed. It was not hard for her to get me to do almost anything and she knew it. So, when her and I went down to the local dance studio and enrolled ourselves in ballroom dance classes, I did have my misgivings. In the back of my mind I somehow thought this was only going to end up with me making a huge fool of myself. I was always fairly athletic, but dancing was something that just never seemed to come natural. Perhaps because my heart was never truly into it. Then again, maybe if I had a partner dressed like those ballroom dancers you see on television it might be a different story.

We paid our dues after listening to a fifteen minute speech by the instructor and headed home. Our classes were to take place every Tuesday night at eight. I had mixed emotions as I drove home that night. For the most part I felt that I really could not make too much of a fool out of myself surrounded by other beginners, yet I still had my reservations.

When Tuesday night finally arrived, Lynn and I drove the

Hot Summer Nights 2014

twenty minutes to the local dance studio. Lynn was much more excited about the whole thing than I was. It would be more accurate to say I was more nervous than excited, though I somehow resisted the temptation to stop at a bar for a few drinks to calm my nerves along the way.

After parking the car we made our way into the dance studio. We were about ten minutes early when we made our way into the big room. It was a sparse room with few adornments other than the folding chairs which lined the walls. People were standing around chatting, waiting for the lessons to begin. Looking around, I counted a total of sixteen people, eight couples in all. Most seemed casually dressed, like ourselves, and my initial impression was that everyone was fairly friendly and easygoing. That was a definite plus.

Several minutes later our instructors walked in carrying a portable sound system which they set up in the front of the room. They were an attractive couple in their thirties, I would guess. Judging from their accents, I would have to say they were from South America. I guess it would be nice to learn Latin dances from real Latin Americans I thought to myself. Later I found out they were indeed from Argentina and had been teaching dance most of their lives.

Carlos and Maria stood in front of the room and gave a brief talk about the different types of ballroom dances following their initial introductions. They had an easy going air about them and punctuated their conversation with occasional laughter. This no doubt helped put everyone at ease, myself at least. When their talk was over they followed it with a demonstration of the various dances while the music played in the background. I could not help but be impressed by the ease of which they glided across the dance floor as us sixteen students stood back and looked on.

After the talk and demonstration, the sixteen students were divided into groups of four, two couples per group. This made it easy for one of our instructors to spend time with each of the groups and it also allowed us the opportunity to switch partners within the group. Lynn and I were paired off with an attractive couple who introduced themselves as Ron and Jillian. I would have to say Jill, as she called herself, was around my age or slightly younger. Her husband Ron was about ten years older than her.

Ron and Jill seemed a pleasant enough couple, which was nice since we would be working closely with them for the duration of the lessons. Ron was by far the most talkative of the two, a very gregarious sort of guy. He informed us that he is a vice-president of a major investment bank. Jill apparently spent her days involved in charity work. One only had to look at her expensive yet tasteful jewelry and

Hot Summer Nights 2014

clothing to imagine a woman whose biggest worry was how to donate the couple's excess money.

Lynn and Ron's shared gift of gab assured there was never a lull in the conversation. Jill by contrast, had a quiet reticence which would seem a put-off to some. She rarely seemed to look you in the eye, but when she did her big brown eyes displayed a remarkable intensity. Far from being put off, I was quite intrigued.

Our instructors made their rounds as we were given some basic waltz steps. Lynn and I moved easily to the rhythm of the music coming from the portable stereo. Carlos and Maria's easy going manner helped me relax and I was able to get into the groove more than I would have expected. Lynn was more of a natural and needed little coaxing.

After a period of time, we were instructed to change partners. It was my turn to dance with Jill. I walked up to her and offered my hand. She accepted and we began to move together in time to the music. This quiet, reticent woman seemed to somehow come alive on the dance floor. Those eyes which seemed so intense yet distant otherwise, took on a certain playfulness. Her curly brown hair framed a face which began to reveal a newfound joy. It was as if someone had taken a key and unlocked a cell door which had been imprisoning her very soul.

As we moved around the dance floor, our movements

locked in rhythm. It was as if time stood still as this otherwise reserved woman seemed to somehow come alive in my arms. Watching a certain glow unfold across her pretty face was causing me to have feelings which were best not shared with Lynn.

That night, on the way home, Lynn and I discussed our first dance lesson. We both agreed that taking dance class was a good move. Lynn and I thoroughly enjoyed our first class, though perhaps not for the same reasons.

The rest of the week, I could not get Jill out of my mind. I sat at work thinking about the girl who mysteriously came alive on the dance floor. Sitting there, I was truly looking forward to my next dance class.

As time went on and our dance lessons progressed, we gradually got to the Latin dances. I was admittedly looking forward to the Rumba, or Argentine Rumba as our Argentine instructors so properly called it.

Lynn took to the Rumba like a fish to water. It was fun dancing with her as her moves were always light and fluid. Her natural athleticism always shined through on the dance floor and her Rumba moves were certainly no exception.

When it came time to dance with Jill the experience was quite different as our hands joined and our fingers touched.

Hot Summer Nights 2014

Whereas Linda was playful, Jill was passionate. Jill displayed a fire in her eyes as she took to the dance floor. Our instructors had explained the Rumba is a seduction of the hips, and Jill seemed to know this instinctively. Her movements were truly seductive as she moved her hips at times with animalistic abandon. It was as if a fire inside was causing her blood to boil. At times, our hips would move together locked in rhythm as if we were joined. It wasn't as if she just enjoyed dancing, it was more as if she truly needed to.

When the dance was over, we both returned to our original partners. Lynn came over and grabbed my hand trying to get my attention. My mind was, however, a million miles away. As I watched Jill morph back into her usual reticent self, my thoughts could not help but start racing through my head.

On the way home in the car that night, Lynn asked me if I thought Jill was attractive.

"Yes, she is an attractive girl." I replied, "Ron is certainly a lucky man."

At least I didn't lie. I was certainly being honest with both my statements. Jill was most certainly an attractive girl and Ron was indeed a lucky man. If she came alive so passionately on the dance floor, I can only imagine in my wildest dreams what she might be like in the bedroom.

A couple of weeks later, it was announced there would be a big party when the classes came to an end. It would be a dress affair at a fairly posh hotel in the area. It would be a chance for all of us students to show off what we had learned in a more proper environment. There would be a real band playing music as well. Besides that, there would be good food and drink. Sounded good to me.

Lynn was really looking forward to the event and I was as well. She went out and bought a new dark blue dress for the occasion. Women generally don't need a good reason to go out dress shopping, but this was indeed a good one. I would wear a dark blue suit I had so that we would sort of match. It was her idea.

The night of the party, or more correctly the ball, soon arrived. Lynn looked so good in her dark blue dress, with her blonde hair and blue eyes that almost matched. I was really quite proud to be seen with her as we made our entrance. She really did look that hot.

The ball was held in a very posh, but aging, hotel not far from the dance studio. There were several banquet rooms but we soon found the correct one. I was really quite taken aback when I entered the room. There was a band playing and sharply dressed waitresses serving drinks. Everyone in the room was dressed to the nines, the men looking rather sharp and the women quite lovely in their dresses and gowns. The old banquet room itself was extremely ornate, with large crystal chandeliers hanging from the high ceilings. The whole effect was quite spectacular and rather breathtaking.

We soon found Ron and Jill and made our way over to their table and took our seats. We had a good view of the band and the dance floor from where we were sitting, but it was the view at the table that caught my attention. Jill was dressed in a satin black dress that highlighted her dark brown hair and big dark eyes. The diamond earrings that dangled seductively from her ears as well as the diamond necklace she wore provided a sharp contrast to this darkly dressed, mysterious woman. She was in her usual pensive mood and one could not help but wonder what went through her mind.

Ron and Lynn more than made up for any lull in the conversation. Both could talk more than a Southern senator during a filibuster and one would have thought they were long lost friends who had recently reunited. I managed to slip a word in edgewise on occasion, but for the most part left the conversation initially to the two pros.

After the elegantly dressed waitresses brought around trays of hors d'oeuvres and took our drink orders, the band took a break. Our hosts, Carlos and Maria took up position prominently in the middle of the dance floor and each made a small speech. It was basically the usual canned speech about how good we all look, how proud they are of us, how far we have all come, that sort of thing. After the speech, Carlos explained how there would be a waltz during cocktail hour followed by dinner. Following dinner would be the Latin dancing where every couple would get a chance to show off their stuff.

The band resumed its playing as Carlos and Maria began the dancing. I took Lynn by the hand as I spoke.

"Waltz, my dear?" I asked with a grin.

She just smiled as she rose from her seat and followed me onto the dance floor. Ron and Jill soon followed and momentarily the whole room was out on the floor waltzing to the music as the band played on.
As Lynn and I waltzed around the room, I was proud to be dancing with such an attractive woman. Yet, I could not help but glance over to Ron and Jill from time to time. That mysterious woman in the black dress with the diamond earrings sparking in the light of the big chandeliers was just something I could not resist taking a peek at. The way she somehow came alive on the dance floor as she moved in time to the music held an indescribable attraction.

Hot Summer Nights 2014

When the waltzing was over we returned to the table and resumed sipping champagne until the food was brought out. The food was quite delicious and wonderfully presented. The food was in fact so good, it was almost enough to draw my attention away from the elegantly dressed women with whom I was sharing a table. Both looked so beautiful as the glow from the candle lit centerpiece and the soft lighting of the old crystal chandeliers lit up their faces.

Following dinner, the plates were cleared and the waiters came out with our coffees and dessert. As we were sitting there eating our mousse, Carlos and Maria again made an announcement from the center of the dance floor. The Latin dancing would soon begin. Immediately following the announcement, the band resumed playing. This time the music had a lively Latin beat. I finished my coffee, stood up and looked at Lynn as I spoke.

"Rumba, my dear?" I asked, extending my hand to her.

Lynn took my hand as we once again made our way out onto the dance floor. The music was loud and lively. You could actually feel the pulse of the music in the vibrations of the old floor boards beneath your feet. Lynn and I joined hands and began to dance the Rumba along with the other students from our class. As we moved on the wooden floor, our hips pulsed and swayed in erotic movements in time to the music. Our movements formed a rhythm that often seemed to lock us together as one. Lynn looked so hot in her blue dress as we moved rhythmically along with the other sweaty bodies on the floor.

After a couple of numbers, Maria made an announcement that it was time for each couple to show off their stuff by coming up to the center of the floor and performing their best moves for a couple of minutes. Because of their position on the floor, Ron and Jill were among the first to take their place in the center.

Jill looked so seductive as Ron led her around on the floor. As the music pulsed, the two dancers moved their hips to the rhythm. Jill looked so good in her black satin dress which had a soft sheen under the light of the old crystal chandeliers. As their movements progressed, Ron spun her around and their number ended with Jill arching her back, her head down with her curly brown hair nearly touching the wooden floor. Ron held her firmly by her thigh as she extended her left leg upwards, toes pointing towards the ornate ceiling. I was finding it quite arousing just watching this normally reserved woman let loose on the dance floor in a very public way. It was a transformation that was captivating and very sensual. My gaze was transfixed, I could not help but stare.

When it was our turn, I took Lynn by the hand and led her to the center of the dance floor. We started our dance as the

Hot Summer Nights 2014

others looked on. We moved in time to the music, our hips swaying seductively to the erotic rhythms. Lynn looked so hot in her blue dress with her blonde hair shining under the soft lights. Yet, my mind seemed to be elsewhere.

Our number ended in a far less dramatic fashion than that of Ron and Jill. We made our way off to the side and stood there watching the other dancers. After every couple did their solo thing in the middle of the floor, it once again became a bit of a free for all. The progression of time combined with the open bar was making for somewhat of a real party atmosphere. Lynn was in a great mood and wanted us to make our way back out onto the dance floor. Just as I was about to join her, I could feel my cell phone vibrate. I unhooked it from my belt and looked at the number. It was my boss John. Lynn looked at me and smiled as she spoke.

"Let me guess, it's your boss John," she said loudly above the music.

"Who else?" I answered somewhat nonchalantly.

It was not unusual for John to call me at night. He is a workaholic who typically works 14 hours a day. The fact that it was after ten did not surprise me. I told Lynn I would be back in a bit. I had to leave the room since there was no way I could call him back and hear anything he had to say over the noise of the band and the people.

I left the banquet room in search of a relatively quiet place to make the call to John. He probably can't find some file which is right in the middle of his cluttered desk. As soon as I left the room, I found another banquet room right next door that was not being used. It appeared to be under renovation as most of the tables were covered with large drop cloths. I sat down in an old chair and admired the dark wood paneling and ornate decorations on the ceiling. Like the room we were in next door, this room had the huge crystal chandeliers hanging down from above. The hotel was really quite old and I could not help but think that it was not often that you see rooms this ornate these days. Even though the band was in the room next door, you could feel the vibrations in the old wood floor.

After completing my phone call to John, I put away the phone and laughed to myself about the trivial matters that my boss feels the need to call me about at ten at night. I sat for a moment in the darkened room which was lit only by the light entering from the doorway. Moments later I rose from my seat and decided to return to the party next door. It was obvious they were having a good time. The music and occasional shouts and laughter could be heard through the old walls.

As I arose from my seat and made my way to the doorway,

Hot Summer Nights 2014

I realized I was not alone. Standing in the doorway was a figure cast in shadow, lit only from behind. The backlighting sparkled in her diamond earrings which dangled seductively from her ears. A small amount of light reflected off a large mirror hanging on a wall delicately illuminating her face. In the near darkness I thought I could detect a faint smile.

I stared into her face intently as the Latin music could be heard faintly coming through the old walls. For a moment, time seemed to stand still as my thoughts raced through my head. Other than the music and the occasional sound of the revelers next door, we were quite alone in that old room. I looked into her big dark eyes as I spoke.

"Rumba, my dear?" I asked softly.

I held out my hand and Jill took it in hers. I led her gently into the old darkened room. We began to dance to the Latin beat coming through the walls from the room next door. Our hips began to move together rhythmically in time to the music as we made our way across the empty dance floor arms intertwined. I spun her around as the old floor vibrated beneath our feet. As the music came to an end, Jill dramatically bent back and extended her left leg up in the air, her curly brown hair nearly touching the old floor boards.

With her leg up in the air, I held her tight by her thigh. I pressed her gorgeous body against mine as my arousal started to grow. Our groins pressed together, I began to stroke her soft thigh. She let out a soft moan as her back arched further, putting her head almost to the floor.

With my right arm around her leg, I placed my left hand under her butt and lifted her over to the table. I laid her down gently on the cloth that was covering it. I leaned over her and gently kissed her on the lips at first, then parted her lips with my tongue as our tongues met. With my hands, I gently fingered her moist lips through her panties before removing them and tossing them on the floor.

Jill reached forward and helped me undo my pants and drop them. I pulled down my underwear unleashing my fully engorged member. I slipped my hands under her black dress which was now pulled up. I gently ran my fingers down towards her womanhood as I kissed her inner thighs. I softly stroked her pussy lips in a teasing manor and lightly encircled her engorged button. With her back on the table cloth, I lifted her feet all the way up onto my shoulders as the band resumed playing. I slowly entered her as our hips joined in rhythmic motion as the Latin music could be heard through the old walls. On that table in that old banquet room we did our own style of dance as the revelers next door could be heard shouting over the music. As we came together in that empty room, our own cries of passion were heard only by the old crystal chandelier and dark paneled walls.

When it was over we sat for a moment savoring each other's company before gathering our clothes and making our way back into the next room. Nothing more was ever said between us and Jill and I never saw each other again.

I just felt I needed one last dance.

11-05-09.

Alan W. Jankowski

http://www.innerchildpress.com/alan-w-jankowski.php

The Erotic Poets & Writers

Call Girl 101

Steve Rawlings liked the girls Sarah Ford supplied him with better than the regular call girls you contacted on the internet or Craig's List. They were women from local universities who needed to make extra money and would turn a trick once or twice a month for ready cash. His friends said they were natural, genuine, and liked to talk. He found them personable interesting. At a recent party with four friends, he asked Sarah to attend and bring someone along. She brought Raddha Desai, whom they knew from previous experience. She also brought Jancinda Lamott. "It's her first time," Sarah explained "you don't have to pay her. I'll give her something from my money. She's checking it out to see if she wants to go with it." Everyone wanted Sarah, who was a tall track runner with red hair topside and below decks; and Raddha, with her beautiful coffee-cream skin, jet back hair, and lithe body. Tobias took Jancinda to bed. A couple of days later Steve asked him how she was.

"Best fuck I ever had," Tobias said. "She's short, but my God, she's got the stuff—a real little hell cat."

Steve arranged a coffee date with Sarah later that week.

"This Jancinda—does she want to throw in?"

"She said maybe once or twice a month."

Hot Summer Nights 2014

"Does she go to GVSU?"

"Calvin."

Steve laughed. Calvin College was a religious school. "I'd like a girl for the weekend. If she's available, I'd love to have Jancinda. It will be the usual. Friday night to Sunday morning."

"I'll check with her."

An hour later, Sarah called.

"It's good I'll drop her off at your place at 5:00 on Friday."

****

Jancinda Lamott arrived on time. Sarah never came along with her girls when she dropped them at a client's house. He met her outside, in the garden by his swimming pool.

She *was* short—maybe 5'4", and had dark hair and brown eyes. Tobias was right, though. She definitely filled out the little black dress she had put on for him. She would be worth the money.

"Jancinda," he said. "That's a cool name. It's different."

"My Mom had a thing for odd names," she answered. "I have a brother named Thaddeus. He lives in Houston."

"What does he do?"

She smiled a crooked smile. "He scores drugs. My brother is a crack head. I don't even want to think about where he gets the money to score. And you, Steve? Sarah says you run a successful start-up company."

He gave her some details. His web company had taken in three million last year he had carefully expanded and looked to double profits this year.

"Very cool," she said.

"Well, I thought we might go to a nice restaurant"—

"I think we ought to fuck each other first," she interrupted. "There will be a lot of tension hanging in the air until we do. So let's get it on. I want to be able to enjoy the meal." She paused a moment and smiled. "Sarah told you I'm new at this, I imagine."

Her response rattled him but he nodded.

"Well, I'll be worrying about what you might think about me and won't be able to appreciate wherever you take me. So first things first."

Hot Summer Nights 2014

"Sounds good to me."

He led her to his bedroom. He noticed she had a small suitcase with her.

"Is there a place where I can change?" she asked.

He pointed to a room off to one side of the master bedroom—a guest bedroom. Carrying the bag, she disappeared inside and closed the door.

He turned the lamp low, got undressed and waited, inexplicably feeling anxiety, a thing he never felt with Sarah or any other women he had hired out for a weekend. After ten minutes or so, Jancinda came back into the room. She had put on black thigh-highs and a sheer black top. He admired her breasts, large with small, dark nipples. Her body, toned and muscular (Sarah said she played an endless round of sports) sloped down to a nest of black hair between her legs. He could see her opening and admired the way her strong legs lifted up her cunt and ass. She slid into bed beside him. They kissed.

"I like your outfit," he said."

"I thought if I was going to play the part I might as well look the part."

He might have asked her to elaborate her comment, but lust had taken over him, his cock was hard, and he could not restrain himself even if he felt he should talk to her more. He took her in his arms and kissed her, running his hands over her ass, probing her opening with two fingers. She was wet, which surprised him a little—but then he remembered she was not a professional. He spread the sticky fluid from her vagina on her nipples and then licked it off, which made her sigh and wiggle. He kissed her lips, neck, and shoulders; her breasts and stomach and went down to lick her cunt. She trembled and moaned. He gently rolled her on her back and got a condom out. She watched as he put it on. He asked if they needed lotion.

"You got me pretty wet," she said, "but just a little maybe."

He lubricated the lips of her vagina, feeling the heat on his fingers, took her in his arms, got in position, and pushed into her.

He began to fuck her with a hard, rhythmic motion. For a moment she was quiet and passive, but soon he felt her move and start to make noises somewhere between cries of joy and grunts of determination. Jancinda rotated her hips. Soon she moved her body in a slight figure-eight motion, matching his rhythm, gasping and crying out, tightening and loosening her pubococcygus muscle, alternating pressure and lightness as he thrust into her. He felt her pussy get wetter—her kisses too. She wiggled so as to maximize pleasure, hooking on leg over the back of his thigh, tightening her arms so her breasts pressed into his chest. Her face came even with his shoulders, so he kissed her hair and her forehead. Their dance of bodies went on, both of them reduced to sighs, squeals, and grunting. He felt her suddenly stiffen and let out a long, low call. She was saying something but he couldn't understand her. When she went off, it aroused him. He felt a tiny spot of pleasure build at the base of his spine and in a moment he ejaculated again and again into her. She held him tightly and wiggled as he went, making passionate noises until they both fell quiet. He rolled off of her. She lay next to him, fingers lightly touching his shoulder and left pectoral. In the well between them under the sheets, her smell floated upward. He kissed her softly.

They lay in the aftermath, saying nothing at first. Soon a conversation started. They showered together and got dressed. They fell into shop talk: business, start-ups, banking, investments, and the stock market. Oddly enough, Steve hardly got to talk on such things. His associates did not want to give the impression they were lecturing him or trying to influence his decisions, so they avoided subjects related to business. He took Jancinda to San Chez Bistro. They talked incessantly. After the meal they went to a bar, met up with some of his friends, drank until late, and tumbled into bed and to sleep when they got home, waking late in the morning.

Once they were awake, Jancinda took the initiative. Steve found himself in the passive role as she climbed on him and lowered herself, envaginating him. She settled on him with a low moan, not sitting up but rather stretching herself, her breasts soft on his chest, cheek against his neck, her black hair falling over his shoulders. She put her arms around him and began to move her hips, rolling her cunt, bring her strong, compact body into a counter-rhythm with his thrusting. Waves of pleasure rolled over him. It was nice to have her do most of the work. Grunting and gasping, she put herself to the task of pleasuring him, her pussy getting wetter and wetter, the friction of her body heating him as she moved faster, hair flying, the sound of her back-and-forth increasing, the sweetness and violence of her passion high and intoxicating. She queefed once or twice. He reached down to her soft, round ass, pressing her into him. She came, rocking, convulsing, but not losing her rhythm for even a moment. Ecstasy fell over him like a tide. Her body, compact, strong, moved in a current of delight on him. He sensed the beginning of an orgasm. It exploded. She bore down, tightening her vagina, gripping him as he emptied himself into the condom. He wished they were in the kind of relationship where he would not need to wear one. She lay on top of him a few minutes and then rolled off.

He dozed. When he woke up, she was gone. He smelled bacon and heard the sizzling sound it cooking. He threw on a pair of shorts and went into the kitchen.

Hot Summer Nights 2014

She stood at the stove. Looking trim and athletic in shorts and sports bra, she smiled at him.

"I rummaged around the kitchen to find the breakfast food. Hope you don't mind."

"Not at all."

"I thought I'd cook. I don't like to eat out all the time."

She made bacon, eggs, and toast. They ate and talked.

Her remark about not wanting to eat out all the time led to a discussion of local restaurants. He enjoyed the conversation and found out she had eaten at most of his favorite locations: Marie Catrib's, The Green Well, Seoul Garden, Real Foods Café, Bombay Cuisine. He enjoyed the meal more for the conversation and remembered how dull and boring it had been, even with Sarah, when he had hired other of her girls for an overnight. Sarah was in business management but somehow felt when she was with him she had to do whore-talk. They had never had an engaging talk. Intelligence and energy animated Jancinda's conversation skills. She was not thinking about how soon she would have to give it up for him and wondering when he would pay her and she could go home. She talked because she enjoyed talking with him.

The Erotic Poets & Writers

He told her he had work to do and would she mind if he spent some time on the computer. She shrugged. "Your call," she said. "You're the boss."

Steve did not like the reminder that he was paying for her prostitution services, though she asked himself why he should not.

"I brought some running gear. Would it be okay if I went out for a run while you're working?"

He said it would be fine.

He worked for two hours. He saw her leave in running gear. She returned an hour later, sweaty and droopy (the weather had been humid the last couple of days). Instead of showering, however, she went out to the pool, took off her running shoes and athletic socks, and put her feet in the water. He slipped on his swimming trunks, and came outside, settling into a chair at the edge of the pool.

"Good run?" he asked.

"Miserable," she replied. "It's too humid, but I make it a point to run four days a week." She glanced around her. "Can anyone see inside this fence?" she asked.

He grinned. "I had it built high enough that no one can see in. I had it built that way so you can do what you want to do with no prying eyes."

Hot Summer Nights 2014

He thought she wanted to go skinny dipping, but she walked over, sat down in front of him and began to rub his crotch. He felt himself get hard instantly. She got on her knees. "Take off your trunks," she said.

He obeyed. She leaned forward and took his cock into her mouth. He felt the warmth and gentle pressure. She began, caressing with her lips, running her tongue over and around him. He closed his eyes and felt wet, mild friction and enjoying the rhythm she set. Suddenly she moved forward until he lips were against the place where his cock came out of his body. Eyes bulging slightly, she wigged her head from side to side, paused a moment then backed off with a gagged breath and began to moved again.

Steve felt taken out of his body as Jancinda systematically pleasured him. After five minutes of her sweet laving, he came, dumping load after load into her mouth. She held steady and, when he was done, with a loud slurping sound, let his cock drop out of her lips. He heard her swallow as he opened his eyes. She smiled up at him.

Sarah and Raddha always smiled and said, "Did you like that?" The full-time whores he hired always did something similar, giving him a slutty smile and asking if it was good or if he had ever had a blow job that sweet. Jancinda said nothing. She peeled off her sports bra, shorts, and underwear, and dove into the water. He got his trunks on and dove in after her.

He watched her swim, marveling at how strong she was and how the muscles in her back, buns, and the back of her legs flexed as she propelled herself. She liked to swim underwater. He was amazed at how long she could hold her breath and at how white she looked in the blue chlorinated pool. He asked about it.

"I'm pale," she smiled. "Lots of people with black hair don't have much melanin in their skin. I don't tan, I turn red or burn. It's frustrating."

Her pale, muscular body looked sexy. She swam about like a seal, mostly under the surface, flexing, kicking her feet, coming up to float on the top for intervals, diving down again in a regular sequence. He asked if she had been on the swimming or diving team.

"No. I played basketball and did pole vault in high school, but I always liked to swim and took a couple of swim classes for my physical education requirements."

"Do you play in college sports?"

"No. Too much work, too much commitment. I want to get my degree and get out."

They swam together until he got a call. One of his clients needed to see him. He could tell there was no way around it. He went to her. She stood at the edge of the pool drying herself with a colorful beach towel. He explained what had happened. She grinned and did not seem upset.

"Sarah probably told you what I usually do when this happens," he said.

She nodded. For interruptions during weekends, he gave gift cards to the women he hired and sent them shopping. Steve had not planned to give a card to Jancinda. It seemed too sleazy, though he had not felt this way about any of the girls he had hired before and given cards to—more than one of Sarah's girls. Jancinda seemed to sense his discomfort.

"Would you like to go shopping?" he asked.

"Sure I would. I can always use clothes. And Sarah's not picking me up until tomorrow."

He nodded, dug through a drawer, and found a gift certificate for $300.00 at one of the high-end clothing stores in town. He said he could drop her off there.

Steve drove away after letting Jancinda off in front of the clothing store. He had thought about telling her she could go home and dropping her off wherever she lived, but Sarah maintained strict rules for that. She gave her women rides to clients and picked them up. They did not drive themselves and did not ride home with their customers under her governance. "Why not?" he asked once.

"It's a business transaction, and we keep it that way."

He did not fully understand her reasoning but accepted the conditions. He would pick Jancinda up at the boutique at 5:00.

The meeting turned out profitable and necessary. If he had not met with this associate he would have lost money. Luckily, it ended at 4:30. He drove over to find Jancinda sitting on a bench in front of the store. She looked pretty in tights and a smock. On the bench beside her sat three or four large bags of merchandise.

"Did your meeting go well?" she asked as they drove.

"I went okay. It was good I got together with the guy." He paused and asked, "Did Sarah tell me you're an English major?"

"I am but I have a double major in English and business. I want to start a company that does writing—business writing, resumes, grant proposals. I'd like to do an online start-up."

He wanted to give her advice on how to get a start-up running, to build a clientele, advertise and promote. Somehow, though, he could not get the word out of his mouth. The nature of their association barred certain kinds of discourse. He did not know how to discuss business matters with a girl he had hired to serviced him, however much he wanted to. For the first time in his life, he felt inhibition over discussing business matters.

"Have you done that sort of thing?" he asked, hoping his voice did not sound constrict from the nervousness he felt.

"I've done some grant writing. It was successful and the people want me to do more of it. I made pretty good money off it, though not enough." She gave him a look. "Otherwise, I wouldn't be doing this."

Good place for a joke, he thought, or a quip that would make them laugh and break the tension that had built up. But he only smiled. He asked if she wanted to eat at any of the restaurants she had mentioned earlier. She chose the Green Well.

They drove to Cherry Street and found a place to park. A pleasant sunny afternoon, they sat at an outside table. Steve found the courage to ask Jancinda a question or two.

"Do you like Calvin?"

"It's a good school.my family comes from that faith tradition so they said they would pay my way if I attended there. I would have maybe preferred U of M, but Calvin was a free ride."

"Don't you hate the restrictions?"

"Really, there aren't that many restrictions. I mean, you see what I do on weekends."

He laughed. They talked about sports and music after that. Her statement on working as a call girl weekends had made him retreat to reticence once more. He felt nervous and self-conscious about paying for her even, even though she seemed completely fine with doing so. Steve could not understand why he felt the way he did.

They finished their food and walked down to Brewery Vivant for beer. Jancinda said she thought the place was too noisy. They found a table outside, drank, and talk trivialities. Dusk settled over the sky. They headed back just as night had settled in, swam, washing, and went to bed.

Their lovemaking was slow and deliberate. By now he had some sense of her moves and, he supposed, she of his. He rolled on her in long, even motions and she undulated beneath him, matching him with counter-thrusts that ramped up the pleasure of their embrace. He thought he felt her respond with genuine passion, though he could not be certain. After all, he had hired. When the avalanche of orgasmic pleasure buried him, after they had lay in the afterglow of it, cleaned up, and sent fell asleep, he thought of what his sister had said to him.

Lisa was a student at the University of York, Ontario. Once when he attended a motivational conference led by Robin

Hot Summer Nights 2014

Sharma, she took the bus up to see him, visiting him twice in the four days he was there. He had brought Raddha along (she was also a fan of Robin Sharma so Steve had paid her way to the conference). Lisa saw them together.

"You are dating that Indian girl, aren't you?" she asked over lunch one day. He hesitated and she said, before he could speak, "I should have said, you're *paying* her." He sputtered something about how could she know about their relationship, but her hostility cut him. She rolled her eyes. "I've got friends in town, Steve—a couple of friends who work for Sarah Rawlings and say you're one of her customers—a regular customer at what one of them calls the Get Yourself a College Girl Agency. Does this woman—what's her name?—work for her?"

"Her name is Raddha and, yes. What about it?"

"You're exploiting her."

Now it was his turn to roll his eyes. Lisa tended toward conservatism and had scandalized him by informing him George W. Bush got her first vote after she turned eighteen. She was critical of feminists and had had more than one live-in boyfriend.

"You can't exploit someone who is willing. These girls don't need to do this."

"Then why *do* they do it?"

"To get some ready cash working at something they enjoy."

"You wish," she said, sipping her beer and changing the subject. She did not say anything more about it.

As he lay in bed and felt Jancinda's warmth, he thought of how Lisa's challenge had dampened his weekend with Raddha and the motivational seminar. He could never quite dismiss her censure.

He wanted to snuggle against her, but could not bring himself to do so. Even though he felt he was being ridiculous, his feelings persisted. Too intimate a gesture for someone he had paid for sex. He fell asleep on his side of the bed.

*****

They slept late that morning. By nine the sun shone through the windows. He woke up to see her kneeling on the bed beside him. Her short black hair gleam in the light filtering through the curtains. Her breasts, full and white, their raspberry-red nipples a contrast to her pale skin, had crescent-shaped shadows beneath them. Her stomach curved down to the lattice of black hair that crept up from the juncture of her strong legs. She smiled.

"I couldn't find any condoms in the drawer by your bed," she said,.

Hot Summer Nights 2014

He thought he was out. He should have bought a pack.

"I brought some with me," Jancinda smiled. "'Be prepared,' Sarah always tells us, but I was thinking I could do something nice for you this morning that wouldn't require a condom. Are you game?"

He nodded, thinking she would give him another blow job. Instead, she pulled the covers back, stroked him until he was stiff, leaned down and pushed her tits together, enveloping him in the folds of their warm softness.

Jancinda slowly moved back and forth, gently pressing, enveloping his cock in the smooth, hot flesh of her boobs. Steve felt himself lose control, mastered by her envelopment and the even motion of her body. She took her time, seeming to revel in how she had used her body to master him. After several minutes, he felt it build. She moved more quickly and pulled away as deposited a layer of semen on his stomach, as spasm after spasm rocked him. Jancinda resumed her kneeling position when he was finished. He opened his eyes and saw her smile down at him, sunlight on her face and shoulders, on her breasts, light bathing one side of her body.

"I'm going to get cleaned up now. Sarah will be here for me pretty soon."

He nodded. She climbed off the bed, opening her legs so he caught a glimpse of the beauty that lay where they came together. She went to the guest bathroom. He walked to the one he used, cleaned up and changed clothes. The tone of her voice had told him she had performed the services for which he had hired her and now it was time to close the deal. He found the envelopes--$3000.00 in cash for her, $2000.00 for Sarah—thought a moment and put all the money in Jancinda's envelope. He would see Sarah on Monday and pay her then. He put a note in Sarah's envelope telling her as much and adding he would throw in another thousand for the delay in payment.

He heard her in the kitchen. When he came in she had put on a denim miniskirt and a pink blouse. She smiled at him.

"I've sort of acted like your kitchen belongs to me," she said. "Sorry."

"Fine," he answered, noticing she had got out some microwaveable Danish. They breakfasted on these with milk and coffee to drink. He wanted to ask her what she had on her agenda for the week but thought it might be an inappropriate question. They ate mostly in silence. Sarah showed up just as they were finishing. He said good-bye and that he hoped he would see Jancinda again. "You never know," she said, and walked with Sarah to her car.

****

Hot Summer Nights 2014

Steve saw Sarah on Monday, paid her, and arranged for some of her girls to work at a party he had scheduled next month.

"I've got three girls who can make it," she told him and, reading his thoughts, added, "Not Jancinda."

He felt an inward sting. "Why not?"

"She only wants to work once a month. Her parents pay her school costs and she makes quite a bit doing grant writing, resumes, and job letters for people. She plans to start a writing business someday. Did you talk to her about that?"

"A little bit," he lied.

Sarah smiled. "She told me she thought she got an A in Call Girl 101."

He could only say he thought she had.

After Sarah left (with her money for arranging Jancinda's visit), Steve sat down and thought about the weekend. He fantasized calling Jancinda and asking her out on a *bona fide* date. He could tell her about his start-up and advise her on creating her own business. He could find out what books she was reading in her English classes and what he thought were reasonable goals in life and noble aims. Even as he thought this, he knew it would never be. Hiring her had set the limits of their association. It could never be anything different. He somehow knew she would never work for him again. His only consolation, he realized as he sat by his swimming pool in the warming sunlight, was that his sister Lisa had been wrong, if one extended her judgment to include Jancinda Lamott. Jancinda had used him. He was the commodity. She was finished with him. She had put him behind her and no longer had any interest in him as a person. She never really had in the first place.

He sat there in the sun, remembering.

David W. Landrumn

Hot Summer Nights 2014

Hunt for me

When you find me
You will have me
Then grab for me
As if you thirst me
Then gaze maniacally
In my eyes searching
For your temptress
For her you're unearthing
Proclaiming you heard the siren's call
Beseeching the shrouds to remove thy cloth
And only then will her smile spread
Beseeching you to raise your head.
Hastily grasp at her lustrous wake
Seek out the pleasure carved on her face
Make quick with your entry; time is for the weak
Waves surge under temptations heat
Breathless tossels in this bedline war
Itch your being, leave your mark
Quicken the pace, she'll soon reach Trembling nerves at her very peak
Dislocating the woman that was me
Reborn and steadied...
I am your vixen
Your gaze I favour
Rush for my body
It is yours to savour

Alesha Aris

From My Viewpoint

From my viewpoint
you have the legs
which speak and dance
on rivers, and tonight I
just want to drown:
if you were here
over and above my
dark, carnal needs,
then maybe I would
begin to feel young
& full of juice and
slowly coming along to
places you talked about
in your sleep—
come now,
know the rivers
lead along by those
elongated legs,
and let's get to
know those things
clearing my view.

James Moore

Hot Summer Nights 2014

The Lover's Moonlight Serenade

Walking in the moonlight,
Hand in hand,
She was his woman,
He was her man,
Wearing the white of purity,
As their love was true,
He encouraged her to be herself,
Something no other wanted to do,
Feet so bare,
Breathing the ocean air,
Water splashing,
Her womanly silhouette revealed,
He tried not to peeked,
He felt like a heel,
Moonlight illuminates the path taken,
On her golden highlight awareness awakened,
She looks of an angel,
He knows he can't touch,
Longing for a taste,
Her sweet lips in haste,
Aroused by her shiver,
Her body reveals her chill,
He dares to put his arm around her,
But fears his hardness will be revealed,
Falls comfort in his security,
She smiles at him,
She hopes she isn't to obvious,
As she's watching with a grin,
Aroused by his animalistic instinct,
The growing of his man,

The Erotic Poets & Writers

A larger wave splashes upon them,
She feels safe under his guard,
Could he be her life long partner,
Should she jump in with no holds barred,
Tears she has not shed over him,
Except when ill with the flu,
He has earned her smile,
It has been a year,
Should she share her whole self,
This is what many woman do,
She has given herself to men,
Well maybe a few,
It was what was to be excepted,
At least she was pressured too,
But he just protects her,
Making her laugh,
Her love for him true,
She never wants to bid this king adieu,
Silently the couple walks,
Hand in hand,
She his woman,
He her man,
Maybe the pulling of the tides,
Possibly the moonlight,
The meeting of the lovers,
It shall happen in the tonight,
Walking in the water deep,
Being met with chilled peaks,
The taste of salty liquid drips from thy mouth,
Longing for more,
There white garments hit the ocean floor,
Lifting her on his mighty staff,

Hot Summer Nights 2014

Stumbling in the waves,
It made them laugh,
As she slides on,
The two becomes one,
A serious turn this action took,
Eye to eye,
Their bodies shook,
Only being a minute or two,
This was just the beginning,
Though skipping a step,
Another layered sealed this love that's true...

Janet Renee Cryer

http://www.lulu.com/spotlight/jreneecryer

Tempest

A petal falls and comes to float
Upon a lake of placid still.
Like gentle sway of empty boat,
Oblivious to early morning chill.
Upon the surface it skims along,
Mirrored reflection in tranquil glass.
Deaf to melodious dawn chorus-song,
A fleeting moment, come to pass.
The wisps of cloud that streak the sky,
A temperate blessing of heaven's grace.
Glowing glorious, canvas upon high.
Our private, secret dwelling place.
Verduous branches cast cool soft shades
That overhang, their boughs sweet harbour,
Along the shore and leafy glades,
Sheltered seclusion for lover's ardor.
Through dappled light of sunrise-show,
In the gentle caress of playful breeze,
A rustle of countless leaves that glow,
Incandescent bloom of flaming trees.
Where numberless shadows, downward cast,
Dance in merry sun-cast mirth.
An undulating, perfumed viridian mass,
Upon the luscious soft green earth.
Lay with she, her hair a-braid,
Enticing scent of honeysuckle sweet,

Hot Summer Nights 2014

And in the distance, valley-glades,
Swaying fields of golden wheat.
Rising sun with molten gold doth dress,
Two bodies, one head resting soft upon a breast,
That warmth surrounds and affectionately caress,
The steady beating of wanting heart in chest.
Soft lips touch to share honeyed dew,
Flushed cheeks burning as we dined.
Adrift in eyes as passion grew.
Hand in hand, lost fingers intertwined.
Eyes clenched shut as light to dark,
Sight became shadow under nature's shroud.
Scorching fingertips burn hot their mark,
As upon whispered breaths our love avowed.
With each trembling touch our worlds collide.
No breathing soul with heart so warm,
In such serene a place could turn,
A placid heart to raging storm.
Two become one as each become whole.
An irresistible, desperate, aching urge
To consume a beauty of angel, stole
In the frenzied swell of tempest surge.
Where beauty cannot fail to keep
Such radiant eyes from impassioned gaze,
Upon the midnight, perilous ocean-deep,
Pour forth and set the world ablaze.
Heavy cloud as dark as night,
Whipping wind, vicious and feral,

Fingers gripping, fists clenched tight;
Tipping danger in exquisite peril.
Gasping need, storm's breath that roars,
A hot-blooded, intense and fervid capture.
Like violent crash of waves on shore,
An inflamed release of sunrise rapture.
Clutched with greed, the richest treasure,
Blessed be those that feel such bliss.
Sinking into pain and pleasure,
Heaving chest soothed gently with a kiss.
Murmured words of softest light
Calm the waves of turbulent squall.
Opening eyes to dazzling sight,
Embraced by arms to cease the fall.
Like blossom caught upon a summer's breeze,
Rising heavenward, far away they soar.
My heart, my gift for you to seize,
At least forever, evermore.

Elizabeth Jones

Hot Summer Nights 2014

WithInAverage

Sum Come2me 'bout they Big10inch
Talking'MeUp how they'll ScratchMyItch
& i'ma Tellin'U i Don'tNeedNo
SuperStar...in fact, WhatMovesMe is far,
FarFromMeasurable: what i find
PleasurAble is MindLovin'Mine...my mind
Rollin'&Tumblin', Rockin'&Rollin' with
the GreatestOfEase, & the 15CentiMeters of
WithInAverage can please
AsGoodAs--no, Better'nYoQuarter
NoLonger, but shorter, a ShortCut2Glory
InUrEyes is DaPrize: Love'sDaPoint of MyStory…

santiba, aka Su(e)NiaDiyg

The Erotic Poets & Writers

I Want to Make Love to Every Part of You

I want to make love to
every part of you
every angle and facet of
your polished light
from your beautiful purpose
to your passionate ideas
I want to kiss your words
and taste your silences
I want to take your wisdom and pain
into my deepest softest core
I am on fire for this
and when I hold your
magnificent body
tightly to mine
pulling you close, and closer still
it is only because
I want to lean as far
as I can
into the everything
of you

Ann Betz

Hot Summer Nights 2014

Beautiful Lady

Beautiful lady spin your spell

      amuse me with your story.

Come when I call you, sit at my table

      seduce the gaze of all who pass by.

Beautiful lady, walk by my side

      master of all that you do

      hear what I speak, laugh at my jokes

      you delight me with your smile.

Beautiful lady, men stare in awe

      they think I possess many riches.

Only you, beautiful lady, know I am hollow,

      stand by my side 'til I tell you to go.

Ann White

www.CreatingCalmNetworkPublishingGroup.com

Passion Blooms

As embers smolder waiting to ignite,
they reach for the other in the dark of the night.
Hands beginning to explore , creates a
hunger building as they thirst for more,
caressing each other from head to toe,
pushing the lines of how far they can go.
Interlocking their tongues begin twisting,
as their lips greedily continue kissing,
futile are their attempts of resisting,
as clearly their desire are insisting.
In an instant bodies are now bound,
the room now fills with primal sounds,
giving in to their will, simultaneously passion, spills
as lust filled needs are met the night reminds it not done yet,
quivering in each others arms sounding bells of a second alarm,
within their passion again consumed lust once again finds bloom.

Mr O. and Gracey Flynn

Hot Summer Nights 2014

Night Worth Celebrating

That hot summer night
When you held me:
The sky became bluer
The moon more silvery
The songs of the birds sweeter
The air fresher
My senses tossed on
The rising tide of desire
Emotion crackled in my
Heart like a dancing flame
Amusement rained down on
Me like an instant shower
My muscles reacted by
Melting under the pleasure
Of the contact and my feelings
Became Indescribable, unthinkable,
Unimaginable, incredible
Romantic and sweet
Your touch left me besotted
My honey you're the very fabric of
Every lofty vision I had ever
Formed of my ideal woman.

With you in my arms
Words were unnecessary
To say I'm in love because:
Words are unnecessary to tell
A blind man that it's raining
Like words are unnecessary
To tell a deaf that there's war
Just like words are unnecessary

To tell a mad man that the
Market is ablaze
Love's radiations from me
Penetrated places words couldn't reach.

So please come closer because
Any time you're near
My eyes danced in ecstasy and
Your delicate fragrance twine
Through my senses entangling
My mind like a silken rope
Please come closer so that
I can show you how much
I care for you because
Wherever you are there I'll be
Like two peas in the proverbial pod.

Anthony Modungwo

Hot Summer Nights 2014

Just once

I've dreamt of hearing you say it since the first moment we met

Wondering what it would take to release that sound from your mouth

Where would we be when your throat finally made that offering to my ears

Would I be close enough to feel your breath on me as your lips parted

Would my heart skip a beat as the inflection in your voice melts the synapses of my brain

Will I hear it a second time straight away or will u leave me wondering

Just once, I want to feel you say it just once.

Neville Hiatt

All the Women

he arises from his bed of lies
the latest victim still in her motionless slumber
in his thoughts he recalls last night's cries
"Ooh baby, yes daddy, give me more"
he's heard it so many times now he just gets bored
once he learned how to have his way
they'd all give him what he wants just to be his if only for a day
his reckless abandon, nonchalant demeanor, and sensitive touch
he tells each her what she wants to hear until he gets to nut
each one thinks it's just her but they know the truth by and by
he loves them all that's why he doesn't have to lie
he says don't ask me, I won't tell you"
He omits, he relishes in its significance
that is becoming more significant
as he professes his love to all the women, each her
fascinated by her curves, loving her scents
he feels each her is heavenly sent
each body he lays down he wants to conquer
they give his kingship the ability to rule their thrones

Hot Summer Nights 2014

all the women that have touched his bed and forgot about their happy homes
his secrets, their lies, through the sheets and between all thighs
each on different emotional highs
he smiles as they cry
all the women's faces he sees riding him from atop to when he slides from behind
arrays of hues and shades, unique colors and creams
only in the moment of bliss do they stand out thru hollers and screams
all the women

Matt Parker

The Erotic Poets & Writers

Hot Chocolate in the Morning

Nothing warms me like that first sip
when I feel that heat of that sweet flavor upon my lips
as I softly lick them catching each drop
experiencing each delectable drip
between the time when the sun peeks its head out
and the moon has retired swiftly in the sky
I seek the delicate twinkles so brightly filled and displayed
in between those thick warm thighs
the waves of your aroma flies like strings of woven yarn
as I inhale the fumes of the morning made fire
so ready to sample the ripened fruits of my famished desire
so delicious is the taste of that chocolate
the kind that wet the stain of our ruffled sheets
good enough to eat as I lick and then swallow
I must say what a wonderful way
to commence the beginning story of the day
with a bubbling broth there light as chiffon
exposed and revealed beneath the cotton panties
as I slip slowly in between them
seeing the revealed treasure of my meaty morning prize
my my my
that is such a beautiful sight for my ravenous eyes
the fabric moist and damp on the back of my neck
as your thighs part before me like the wetness of the red sea

Hot Summer Nights 2014

as you read me as my words leak long
from the tip of my rigid and ready implement
solid in my conception like the girth of my erection
with the firmness of the highest mountain top
I feel the heat like a warm breath on my cheek
as I lust to lap the lather of your leak
before those sexy undergarments fall in their grace

as I view you in your magnificence from the rear
wishing to immerse myself with the print of my face
for the folds sliding over my open jaw enchant me
flowing through the reminiscing palate
that recalls the nasty naughty adult games
played in the delight of the previous night
untamed thirst has the feeling in the know
of the function of the consenting two
the bond between a man and his brew
the dripping of your foaming frothing morning dew
full bodied you are and so deliciously thick
found in the grinding of those wide curvaceous hips
that are gripped as romantic handles
of the hearty heaping helping of your hot stew
the conjecture of that full flavor
savored in a manner that is beyond measure
as the underwater undercover diver
discovers your hidden forbidden treasure

how I love to smell that enticing scent
wafting through the darkness of the room
a sensuous symbol as if the night has ended far too soon
it was like a kiss had been smelted and melted
then poured in the eternal waiting cup
of the D's of the double you possess
that contain your supple bouncing breasts
which my groping probing palm still seeks to caress
for the stiffness of your nipples
only adds to the ectacy
of this sensuous slurping activity
yet you know this is not my main focus
for it is the container found farther below
where the cream is warm hot and wet
where lovers lick on the waves made slippery and slick

the sprout where the fountain never stops
and erupts so sexy in the erotic carnal context
that becomes so much more to be explored
than the simple definition of simplistic sanctioned sex
I feel the heat flow through my muscles
as if it were forcibly driven
yet the wetness relaxes some of them
while causing others to grow and stiffen
for the throbbing member has a heart beat and pulse
and you can feel it if you squeeze it and listen

Hot Summer Nights 2014

the rigid rod prepares to be delivered
as it is the final dawning spawning gift
as my face enters the bubbling vaginal valley
where those mocha legs that keep my coco warm
they begin to spread ,separate, and slowly lift
and these thick sipping lips I shall give to thee readily
for my breakfast in bed is the breakfast of head
claimed in the poets hungry mouth
that finds the dark sweet pumping pit of honey
and laps it's nectar steadily
as the tongue flickers fast and hot
drenching me in the flawless flavorful flow
found within that sticky clitoris and wonder spot
I ride on the winds of my craving
salivating between your beckoning thighs
unable to see your open moaning mouth
or the rolling of your pretty eyes
as you are ratified and satisfied
from this delicious moment held in time
when the poet not only penetrated
those swollen glowing luscious lower lips
but also entered the depths of your beautiful mind
like the flow of the flowing cup of prose

for my tongue still holds the sweet impressive impression
found in the depths of your coveted chocolate mold

I yearn for the opening flaps of your bottom flower
lapping the petals of that plump and meaty rose
stamped with the licked signature of a unseen seductive logo
where the morning milk of my mahogany maiden
is plundered in the wonder of the mornings know
my desire for it shall never cease
and I could I would sleep peacefully in its creamy crease
in my nasty naughty cup of cumming coffee
released as the new day becomes clear in its dawning
while other lay silent and still are yawning
I am there with you my sexy sassy tasty boo
oh there are so may things I still would love to do to you
for you know my mind and what lies deep inside
that freaky side I hide that loves to eat and ride
the one that grips those hips as they dip and I slide
into another burning deserving succulent serving
of my hot chocolate in the morning

Flowetic Justice – Poem

Hot Summer Nights 2014

Exotica

She is the colors of my emotions, the kaleidoscope of my most intricate fantasies fulfilled, the hues of all that I desire infused within the frame of a single feminine mold made of my mind. The paint of the dawn slides across her writhing form as she lays before me languishing in the streams of infinite indiscretions, a place poured from the deep chalice of the dark channels where my most secret inhibitions are secreted , the naughtiest corner of my lecherous mind where one can find my most detectible visions. This is the domain where the wettest drops of my ink fall in constant display as the descendents of the noble gill of the lollipop wop in their garters and stiletto heels so high, bending and offering their able backsides to the hungry sky, beckoning me to indulge in each savory minute and ever so cute drip that never stops. She soars in the realm where the heaving ships of my seething lust roll hard on the waves of my decadent fantasies as Amazons with no harness and without the obstruction of undergarments seductively steer the helm. They stand in the wide doorway of my demands matching my own impressive height, there before the toggle of my boggling sight, where whips and chains are not instruments of pain but the leave the stains of the most pleasurable of delights. Each sweet color is feverishly unfurled and hurled in the twirls in my illustrious imagination and slip across her naked body covering her from regal head to pretty toe as I bend before her benevolent blend , kneeling before the queen of my erotic steam, as I begin to play and give homage to the perfection of her pastel palace. There in the rubble of my twisted troubles my most titillating tales begin to bubble and are cuddled in the valley of my dormant disasters.

I bow to her as she becomes the master of my madness, the breath of my badness, where the storms are driven from all the ravenous thoughts I keep hidden, sumptuously sealed as I peel back the layers of the lapped labia opening her box as if it were sealed with the tightest brightest ribbon. The purple is the tone of my moaning passion and pulsating bone, the red is the ruby rose crushed in the palm of my thrusting force, the yellow is the mellow of sun kissed wishes of the freaky fellow behind my smile and warm hello, the green is what blooms in the fields of my side so wild where runs the lad who plays in the forests of fondled flesh and meshes with the intents of the consenting and undressed, and the blue is the saturation that ebbs from the banging beds were bodies are damp with the spawning trickles of the hanging threads that conceive the waiting webs of the slickest morning dew. There in the moment between where consultation and conception begins she grins as we partake in the velvet cake baked in the wake of my wants and what she so openly flaunts. Then comes the elation of our beastly fornication as the entire legion of all my varied projected selected feminine figures come and join in bearing the fruits of their upper and lower regions.

I see myself written on the pages of he gaze as she wiggles and commences to giggle as I am immersed in the dispersed answers to all of my most deviant riddles. She is

Hot Summer Nights 2014

the appointed one, the anointed one, who pointed me in the direction found where my insidious ideas have no bounds and the buxom and zesty and breathless and breasty wrestlers of mud grease and oil boil in their tantalizing toil for endless rounds in the playgrounds of my pleasure. What we have is a treasure without measure for she is always there at my leisure. My maiden , my melody, my memory, my mate. My merry vision of voluptuousness and ravishing rendezvous of my most devilish destined dates. The flesh and fur of the fantastic figment of my fantasy come to fruition. She is eternally then and everlasting now forever mine. My Exotica.

Justice Clarke – Prose

Heroes in Heat presents . . .
The Naughty Rise of the Dark Knight

We think we all know them all so well because of the legends of their marvelous deeds. The selfless acts they perform and how they are always there to defend us in the face of evil. We have made them bigger than life due to their fantastic powers that far exceed that of the mere mortals. Weather it is superhuman strength, impossible athleticism and detective skills, incredible speed, of a gift brought on by a mutated strand of DNA, we as a society have always showered them with our accolades for their accomplishments. But what of them and their basic needs. What of the moments when they find themselves less than heroic. After all they are still predominately humans and suffer from the same emotions that we all do . Anger, love, fear, sorrow, fright, and especially lust. These are the now revealed documented personal journals of what happens when those so mighty fall prey to their libidos and our most basic desires. These are the exposed stories that we do not here in the media. These are the tales of *Heroes in Heat.*

Let us begin with an entry from the Dark Knight himself.

I am the one known as the Batman. I am the one they call the Dark Knight. I am the scourge of the criminal world, the figure that strikes terror in the hearts of evildoers, the one who wipes clean the filth from the underbelly of society, and the one who is Gotham's sworn protector . I have been locked here in Arkham City, the massive area turned permanent prison, for weeks now trying to get a handle on the murders that have been happening outside its walls and how they link to the criminal minds sentenced here. I am imprisoned on these dangerous streets with the worst convicts and masterminds of our time yet I am also trapped inside here with *her*. The Catwoman know as Selena Kyle. I had always thought I was able to deal with our unspoken affection and mutual attraction and each time we came close to crossing that line one of us would make that hasty early exit. But in here, constantly seeing her, , being so close to her, I find erotic thoughts creeping into my mind and for the first time I am detecting something I have never felt before. A sensation in my loins that burns hotter with each passing second and that I am finding harder and harder to resist. I am beginning to fear that I have finally found myself in a battle I cannot win, a dilemma with no rational answer, and a trap that has no escape and now way out.

C. William Clarke

The Erotic Poets & Writers

Episode #1- Cat on a Hot Tin Roof

I have been tailing her for hours now watching her every move. I see her slip into a warehouse to pilfer and rob those inside. Not my problem, for its dog eat dog in this ungoverned city. Laws don't apply here and that's fine with me. I have seen her do this numerous times, slide under the security's infrared beams but this time is strangely different. I find myself watching her taunt athletic body. How she leans back, the tilt of her head , the length of her long legs, and how her ample bosom stretches against the fabric of her skintight costume as it points full, high, and proud to the dark night above her. To the Dark Knight above her.

Steamy scenarios begin to dance ion my head and I try to fight off these scandalous images but they force their way into the view of my troubled mind. I can see her there as I am chained in my own batcuffs and she is punishing me for all my sins. Striking me with that whip of hers, that cat of nine tails, as it sails against my receptive and quivering skin . Not hard enough to draw my blood but with enough force to arouse me as I picture her in nothing but a alluring black leather thong that is lost in the depths of her deliciously sculptured backside. I watch her move about this silent desolate structure and my mind begins to play filthy little tricks one me. She leaps , she slides, she jumps,

Hot Summer Nights 2014

she glides , moving with catlike precision throughout the building taking care of the henchmen with violent ease. Seeing her this way only makes me want her that much more. Her raw fury and fighting prowess rivals my own and that has always been an aphrodisiac to me and the source of my tainted addiction to her. Soon in my mind all I am picturing her in is but three remaining pieces of her form fitting attire as I begin to tremble and perspire under my cowl. I see her in simply her mask, her gloves, and her thigh high boots.

I am lost in the lust of my deviant thoughts, captured in the depths of this waking wet dream, until I realize that she is looking at me and smiling. Stunned I turn and fly from the ledge I was perched on. Leaping from it as I glide across the city using my cape as my ever present wings I land and climb high onto the top of an aluminum water tower that overlooks the entire city as I hang my head in disgust. One question echoes in my mind over and over again and I cannot seem to find the answer. A situation I have never found myself in up until now . I ask the question once more but this time I speak the words aloud. "What's wrong with me ?!".

And then I hear her voice as she softly chuckles behind me. Dammit I had forgotten that she was almost as good at tracking me as I was at tracking her. "There is nothing wrong with you my sweet sexy Batman. You are human and finally beginning to show signs of it. I know under all that anger and rage and dedication to justice you are still a man with the same wants and needs of all men and for that matter all women. You want the same thing that I do but are too afraid to admit it. I never thought I would see you afraid of anything ." As she speaks I can see she has opened the front of her costume more than usual, zipped it down for my perusal, so that not only is the cleavage of her large round supple breasts exposed but the circles of her tantalizing aureolas . The crotch of my costume feels like it is going to burst.

She walks up to me and presses herself against me hard and with her wide wet tongue licks my lips and purrs into my ear with her hot panting breath. "You know you want me and you know I want you. Take me, right here, right now. No one will ever know and I can tell by that hot hard strong and long bulge I feel against me that you want this just as badly as I do . For once don't be the Batman baby tonight be the *Bad*man. " I am stunned and in turmoil in my mind and my indecisiveness angers her. "Fine! Go on being afraid but I may not make this offer again!" She turns and strides towards the edge of the tower swaying her wide hips as my eyes fall upon the curves of her beautiful derriere . I lick my lips tasting the flavor of her saliva on my tongue and then I snap.

Hot Summer Nights 2014

I grab her around the waist and let her feel me from behind. No words are needed to be spoken for we have done this too many times in the bedrooms of our minds. Her hand slides down the front of me as her slender fingers fondle the outline of my straining erection. She takes my hand and puts it between her firm thighs as she unzips her costume all the way so that I could feel the wet folds of her throbbing passion pit. My fingers become moist as they play in her dripping folds. I can't wait to do this now. I have hidden these thoughts in the dark recess of my mind for so long and now at last they are about to come to fruition. I want to rip every inch of the skin tight cat suit off of her, so I can sample at my leisure that gorgeous body, starting with the top. I want to release and pounce on those magnificent luscious globes and suckle them like a hungry newborn.

I force her head forward and down. placing my large hand on her back, and stroke her spine to position her properly for my entrance and just like a cat her gorgeous ass raises automatically up in the air. I pull my beating member forth, freeing it at last, and I squeeze it hard in my hand. I am enthralled by the breeze and shiver with delight as I feel the crisp night air blow on it. I sink myself into her juicy mound and she moans low and deep like a cat in heat. I make no sounds for this moment is too profound. I am ashamed at the act that we were committing yet so relieved and grateful as she slides herself back and forth on me and I can hear myself slapping against her bare and bouncing cheeks. The symbol on my chest, which in times of stress becomes a beacon for my safety, cannot handle the rise in my body temperature and glows bright red as if it is in sync with the blood beating through my thumping heart. As for any more details that is all there will be said and except for the spots left by the liquid of our consummation no one could prove that we were ever there. This is just the story of how on one sexy sultry night I shirked my duty and tended to my responsibility of my manhood and her beautiful fat cat booty. And believe me if you saw me as I howled to the midnight moon when I came you would have sworn you never knew me.

This was effect of the lust and fire that flew though me. And trust me, what I speak of is my naughty nasty needy truth. The night the Batman became that Bad Man who made love to the cat on a hot tin roof.

C. William Clarke – Short Story

Hot Summer Nights 2014

Desire

Nose to nose
Lips to lips
Paralyzed in lover's kiss
With intention, praying this will last
Beyond forever into eternity infinitely
Let me taste your skin
I can't get my fill of you
I always want more
My cravings growing
Fangs showing
Ready to suck where blood is flowing
Your fingers trace my spine
Feeling so glorious
Your talents notorious
I take note of how you nibble my ear lobes
Kiss me slow
Make me bend my toes
Caress every inch
Before you inch inside me
I notice your breath as you serve me pounds of love
Hot on my neck
Makes me so wet
I bet we can make love all day
Into the night
Melding together like oil paint
A portrait of beauty
Still
Surreal

Mellenne Carpenter

Sizzle

I sizzle I burn
Stroke upon stroke
I scream as the fire
Takes hold of me
A torch inside me enflamed
I am forever changed
By your kiss.
Your lips reek havoc
On silky skin glistening like dew
My breasts ache to be bathed
By your tongue
As it glids over my creases
My curves
Consumed by a longing
Greater than ever before
I surrender to you
Every fantasy that has
Displayed it's erotic vision
Behind these eyes.
I feel you deep
Still not deep enough
As I can never get my fill of you
We move to an ancient rhythm.
You drink from my passion
Is it sweet?
I thirst for your desire
Smooth salty
I take you deeper still.
We are falling
We are flying
We are the same heartbeat.

Hot Summer Nights 2014

As we hold onto each other
We are now complete
We begin again
For the night has just begun.
This is the first chapter
Pages filled with smoldering passion.
The story of the darkness
Where our bodies danced.
Our heartbeat throbbed
I shall continue to await
Your tender torturous touch
That kills me so sweetly
I wish to die again and again...

Jaz Gill

Close Circuit

Had not this been fragile

I would have positioned

a camera upon my collar bone…

On either side...

And then I would have removed

the extra lenses

one by one

Ah! Such impeccable folds of civilization…

Dr. Kiriti Sengupta

Hot Summer Nights 2014

Blind By Choice

Behind these glasses of darkness

I hide my ravenous gaze-

Lest, every garb on your sweltering frame-

Is furiously set ablaze;

You think I am blind, as inch by inch

You disrobe each night with a careless grin

You're right, I am blind; these eyes were charred

When they first fondled your naked skin;

Ananya Chatterjee

fall apart laughing

the moon robs leaves of their color

as the dead hours

lay waste to the world.

i breathe you in like smoke

and out like soft perfume.

mists of sexual desire

dance on dreams

of burning days.

i murmur enchantments against your skin

as the dangerous beauty of your hands

strokes heaving flesh.

we fall apart laughing

into one soul.

Laura Lee Sugah

Hot Summer Nights 2014

Isla

I woke to the sound of surf in the small, tidy room. French doors opened onto a charming patio, and the next step was in warm dry sand. This two week vacation was a dream come true, a fantasy realized, on Isla de la Paz Hermosa, a small island in the midst of an emerald sea.

It was not a resort in the traditional sense. The decor was serene. The fabric and paint were a light, tone-on-tone brightness. The wood of the furniture was dark and rich. Upholstery invited one to rest in loving and cushioned embrace. There were no televisions, but a library of sorts filled the walls of one long hallway. The music in the bar each evening was soft and sensual jazz provided by a quartet. The atmosphere was only part of the reason I had chosen it. The main factor was its clothing optional policy for beach and pool.

During the first few days I had spent my days on the beach experimenting with the best method to avoid sunburn on tender skin. My skin was now golden and sprinkled with ever darkening freckles. Not a sexy look in my mind, but you get what you get when your skin is fair.

He was on the beach every morning when I walked. His face was bold; his mouth sensuous. I couldn't see his eyes because of his sunglasses. I wondered in my own curious way if he wore them to hide his true self from those who might look too deep. He was comfortable in his nudity and would sit on his towel reading or just watching the surf. I imagined so many things as he sat remote and silent in the bubble of quiet that surrounded him.

There was a storm on the night before everything changed... a big storm. The staff had come to check each room and secure the exterior doors and the patio furniture early in the evening. Their smiling faces and efficient manner did little to assuage my anxiety over the lightning and wind that was forecast. There was a precision about their movements as they assured me that all would be well. I ordered a bottle of wine and prepared for the assault to come.

The roaring storm lasted for several hours. Something kept hitting the glass of my window, but the promises made by the staff held true. My room was secure even from water that might have leaked under the door in a less prepared facility.

I slept fitfully and roused as gray light began to filter through the white gauzy drapes. Birds sang quiet little melodies outside my room. The shower was a welcome balm to body and soul. It is funny how that can be. I slid on a pale pink thong swimsuit bottom which had been my one concession to modesty for this adventure and walked onto the softly lit beach. There was surprisingly little debris, and I actually found it comforting to examine the little piles of flotsam that dotted the pale sand.

He sat close to the water, welcoming the sunrise with closed eyes. One strong, broad hand sensuously stroked his erection as the other cupped his shaved ball sack and caressed his inner thigh. It was like watching a moment of pagan worship. The close-cropped hair and trim body added to the meditative quality. A few pearly drops had appeared on the tip of his penis, and it was all I could do not to kneel before him and lick across that broad head. I willed him to open his eyes so I could truly see him but also feared discovery of my intrusion on such a private moment.

Ragged breath and the swelling blood flow of arousal took control. My legs refused to walk me away or even to support me any longer. I sat tailor fashion on the sand a few feet away. I was snared in his thrall at this point physically and emotionally.

Pulling the heel of my right foot near my butt, I tugged fabric aside and felt the increasing wetness of my slit. My fingers massaged my clit in time with his movements. Skin flushed as I concentrated on his hands and even the movement of the hair on his tanned body.

His fist squeezed and more pre-cum leaked over his hand. He lubricated his shaft and stroked faster. The finger of the other hand teased his anus. My whole body was absorbed by this one man, at this beautiful now, and on the feel of our hands bringing us closer and closer to some metaphysical unity.

I wondered who or what he was thinking about as he stroked.

A small moan caught in my throat as I slid two slim fingers inside my swollen and juicy pussy. His eyes slowly opened, but even the momentary panic could not motivate me to flee. His eyes made me think of a northwestern rain forest... brown and green and cool and peaceful and dangerous and wonderful.

He watched my movements as I watched his. The intimacy was overwhelming as I fucked myself deeper and faster and with complete abandon. I worked my clit with my other hand as I sat in paradise with a lover whose name I did not know.

Hot Summer Nights 2014

We came at roughly the same time. Eyes locked as the aroma and sound and sensation united us. We sat for stunned seconds just looking at one another.

I got on my knees and felt sex dripping down my inner thighs. I crawled across the sand feeling feral and feline. The spell was strong, and I wiped my face across his belly smearing his cum across my cheek. My tongue lapped at his navel, tasting him. I did not know if the groan I heard was his or mine.

I kissed his mouth, got slowly and unsteadily to my feet. The silent sun glinted on wet sand and bodies as I walked away.

Laura Lee Sweet

A Guiding Hand

Her hand is upon mine with power no other hand can evoke
As she instils a sense of smoothness which I acquaint
With the kind of genius existing in a master brushstroke
From an artist who is empowered to rule with paint.
The feel of her gentle touch is pulsating through each vein
As creative strands are emerging inside my brain.
Her hand endows me with the skill to form the trunk of a tree
With diverse strokes of brown color which blend in harmony.

As I mix blue and yellow to form the color green,
Her hand is leading mine back to the canvas as a guide.
The sight of leaves sprouting up is beauty most serene
Complimented by a set of branches which spread out wide.
With Beauty's touch endowing me with skill I apply
Upon diverse parts of a canvas, I begin to paint the sky.
From out of a cloudless blue, the sun has now emerged
Upon a masterpiece where strands of Beauty have converged.

Jason Constantine Ford

Hot Summer Nights 2014

Blind Bind

Ice

A touch of fire

The droplets

Raise heat along the skin

And you withdraw

Only to be forced

To cage your tongue

Behind clenched teeth

My breath follows the moisture

Dragging tension

Lapping the flavor

Pooling under the silk ties

Binding you to me at wrist

The sweat that had collected

At the joining of shoulder blades

You relax behind hidden eyes

Feeling my softness pressing

Into your back

Massaging your spine

A shivering wildness at your hip

I can smell the essence of you

Tightening smooth muscles

Flexing and relaxing in turn

And you know I am near

I can never resist a touch

A kiss, a suckle at bottom lip

A long lick across your chest

Moans speed my attention

To other exposed skin

Gently, softly

Kneeling before desire

Breath heated by ice

Cooled by liquid fire

And it is hard to tell

Who is bound to what

And what binds whom

This is what I want

The liquidity of sodium

Smooth as molasses

With minimum assistance

Save the willingness

Of need to be released

Gail Weston Shazor
© NP 06/03/14

Hot Summer Nights 2014

Joyride Of A Lifetime

She strolled upto the fence, pigtails fluttering in the wind, Samantha hanging onto dear life by her left hand; the curiosity of an eight year old ,to overlook beyond the fence. He looked up too, dismounting his bicycle immediately and waving happily at his new "friend". She of course, snobbish with her Mumbai "airs", didn't reciprocate in the same manner , but instead waved Samantha's palm back at him. He was grinning cheek to cheek and invited both his visitors to cross over into his garden. She looked behind her without heeding, and saw the movers monotonously unloading their belongings from the trucks; her parents supervising them at a distance. The Sun was higher now , and she felt hotter. She pulled her hat nearer her face and quietly walked away.

The same evening , as they were seated at their dinner table, they had surprise guests of their new neighbours. It was the impish boy from across the fence , and a gentleman with him. " Jasnaam Dolat," the gentleman introduced himself, while shaking hands with her father , a stout , dark , humble scientist , who had recently resigned from his government post to start his own pharmaceutical plant, here in Delhi. " Hanumant Joshi, glad to meet you. Please join us for dinner, we have some simple dishes here."

She could see the boys' eyes lit up at the prospect; a disgusting trait she thought, as her own mother would often admonish her if she ever happened to enjoy the meals off other kids' tiffins at school. What could such a boy be named she wondered? " Randeep, boy say hello !" , his father prompted him. " And this here is Sanjita," said Mr. Joshi. She learnt by and by, he had no mother, and that she had passed away in a tragic accident some months ago. This aspect of his life mellowed her a bit towards him. " This is my mother, " he had showed her his locket one afternoon, as they lay under a tree. " Copy of his mother!" she had been amazed.

They started poking sticks into ant-holes, giggling at their adamancy to make a detour, but still find their path home. That game had subconsciously taught them, that when you are passionate about something, nothing should deter you from attaining it...

They got up , with a new idea to celebrate their newly acquired lesson-plant a lemon tree! Sanu ran to her refrigerator, returning with a lemon in hand. He squashed the pulp with a few jumps, and picked up the seeds. Together they sowed them in the soil, deciding to take turns to water it. " This is our tree of friendship !", they chimed in innocent unison.

How the seasons passed into years, how the sapling grew into a sturdy tree bearing coy white blossoms , that dangled with the breeze ! The scent of lemons permeated the air , as though Nature had conspired to keep Ranu in Sanu's mind 247, and vice versa.

Hot Summer Nights 2014

"Sanu!", he yelled, "are you coming or should I leave?"

" Coming!" she hurried, a book nearly about to slip out of her grip in the haste. He kick-started his bike and off they were on their road to college." And haven't I told you too, that you may leave without me if you're in such a hurry!". She wasn't letting him get the better of her. Her terse remark , so unlike her sweet self, made him overlook the bump that was coming, leaving him off balance and sending the bike and its riders into a dismantled heap!

The initial sting of the fall was jolted to oblivion , when they discovered themselves into each others' arms , embraced and glued together.The awareness of their touches sent a zillion sparks bursting in every cell of their bodies. The freshness of it, the sensational zestiness- it was all inexplicable. They managed to straighten up by and by, and also lifted the bike up . They mounted on it silently, a bit tensed even. The rest of the ride was silent upto her college. Just before she got off, he adjusted the rear view mirror to glance at her; she noticed and blushed slightly. " Take care," he said ,as usual, but today it sounded as tough he really meant it.

She saw him waiting in the afternoon, early , like always from his way back from his office, to pick her up from college, before going home. They were in a better mood than morning , and even giggled together at jokes they cracked while passing people. When he left her home , she waved good bye and touched the rim of her spectacles; something she did when in deep thought...

The next day , there he was, smiling impishly- it reminded her of the first time she saw him, in his garden, asking her to cross over. As she walked towards him, she felt the warm tingling of pricks on her cheeks, and heard her heart step up its beats. They were closer today, the distance of childhood had been crossed, and a realization of their attraction for each other allowed her to slip her hand onto his crotch occasionally while he rode on. She was wearing a perfume today, quite unlike her . "Nice fragrance!", he teased her knowingly, and instead of taking him on, she just let it pass with a soft laughter.

As they reached her college, she complained," I don't want to go to college today , please Ranu,". " Since when has studious Sanu started playing truant?", he further teased her. He knew very well , her dedication towards her studies, the aspirations of her parents from her, the background of her very well educated family - a Brahmin Maharashtrian middle-class family who placed great value on academics as their only source of recognition.

"Not today , please , just not today, " she promised. " Okay, let's take us for a joyride then!!", He made a turndown while saying this, his own enthusiasm for all things fun mounting, the son of a wealthy businessmsn, showered with abundance since childhood, all he lacked was attention and care ...He pumped up the volume of his favourite track

Hot Summer Nights 2014

on his i-pod , and a couple of bunny hops down the road she was shrieking like a banshee with glee!!

That evening Mrs. Joshi noticed a change in her daughter's demeanor and meant to mention it to her husband at the earliest instance. " Sanu has grown up now!" she said, the same evening when he returned home from wotk." Do you think , I'm a fool? Or you take me to be blind?", he replied in his usual dog-chases-cat fashion."I wasn't the topper in my batch for nothing! I have already found a match for Sanu in Dhanesh Lele, a Cambridge qualified MBA , working in Global Pharma, son of my close associate Anand Lele.They will come next week to meet Sanu...till then let there be peace..." the last words were spoken in a rush to resume reading the papers.

The lemon tree stood alone today, waiting for either one to come and water it as was the deal between them.But none were forthcoming. Where were they ? Blissfully ignorant, wrapped in each others' hug , they didn't imagine they had come farthest away on their escapades today. Suddenly , the clouds crackled, as though inspired by their getaways to try some backflips and tailwhips of their own!

The lovebirds were sent fleeing for shelter as the skies broke loose, islolated from all mankind into a cavern they could call their own. Once there , they found solace in the arms of one another till the magic began. The only spectator to their passionate orchestra was an owl perched above, who added chorus of hoots to their animalistic grunts, growls purrs , hisses, mooing moans , screeches and gasps...

When the Sun shone again, it brought in a new sunlight into their worlds , one in which they had known the joyride that darkness had taken them on. The way back home was never so reluctant, the rubbing of her soft curves against his solid flats never as gratifying...They exchanged looks which only they could decipher, as they dismounted the bike and went to their respective homes.

"Sanu, where have you been?? I have been looking for you, there has been a thunderstorm! Now go and change, look at you all drenched...", her mother marched her off. Changed and refreshed she sat down at her study- table, recalling all that had surpassed that afternoon. She blushed a couple times, then set herself to her studies.

She was ready the next day, only to see a new car and chauffeur waiting at the gate. "Sanu, we have arranged a car to bring you to college from now onwards. You should stop talking to boys now...you are no more a girl!" " Good morning," she giggled to herself, but dared not to let her mother see her expression. " Did you say something?", she investigated.

As she seated herself within, her eyes looked about helplessly for him. She was very distracted today during all the lectures, fidgety to go home as soon as possible. She wanted to meet him, see him , talk to him. There had not been a single day past ten years , when they had not met or spoken to each other.

She dialed his number. " Hello", he responded from the other end. He sounded perturbed too.

He told her about how her parents had come over to invite his father for her engagement ceremony, how while leaving, her mother glanced askew at him , as though warning him to keep distance from her daughter, how their relationship will only lead to futility, how their match is impossible, the inter- caste issues , the objections ...A Brahmin vegetarian girl , a Jat Punjabi meat-eating boy , the inacceptance from both sides , the prospective oppositions...he wouldn't want her to go through all this hell. He hung up...

She walked towards the car, letting the facts hammer themselves in. As she entered her home, she saw her mother serving coffee, and an unknown lady, quite well-dressed and a formal behaviour, seated beside her. " Come Sweetheart, just in time," her mother greeted her. " This is Sanjita, or Sanu as we call her." The lady nodded in appreciation. " Hello aunty, " Sanu gave her salutations. "Sanu, soon you should be addressing her as mother instead of aunty", her mother informed her lovingly . She moved towards her room listlessly, lifeless rather.

Once alone, she sat down to grieve her loss. But she had a partner , who wanted to share it ; Samantha from the cupboard was looking into her eyes. She took her down, hugged her, and cuddled up to her in bed, drifting slowly into dreamland. She dreamt of a knightrider, he reached out for her and lifted her onto the back seat. She tried looking at his face, but it was masked beneath a dark helmet. She saw the trees brushing past as they rode on, the birds singing songs of melancholic love above them, the mountains dressed in their bright green coats, all were enchantingly pleasant ...till they reached the dead end of a cliff.

The rider stopped his bike, asked her to get off, which she obliged, then without further warning did a 360 Degrees and then sped off the cliff !! She sprang out of sleep, and found herself in a puddle of her own perspiration. She felt hungry. She went down to the refrigerator, and heard the start of his bike. She rushed out, only to catch the mud thrown up in the air, as he raced away.

That had been her last attempt at trying to get a glimpse of him. He showed up himself, dressed in a smart formal suit on the day of her engagement, smiling as always.

Meghna Gupta Jogani

Hot Summer Nights 2014

Suck Sex Fully = Successfully

From a 5 story burning building
I want to free fall with buoyancy
Into your arms like a fire safety net…
Smoldered in affection….
…Extinguish me in kisses

I want to hear your husky voice
Whisper my name like an incantation
And relish over every crevice of me
…Until our bodies were so entwined
That even with the contrast in skin color
We'd be hard pressed to tell who's who

Listen to me….
With your eyes for the reason that
I speak many dialects…
I communicate with body language
And will talk in tongues for you
Perhaps I can suck-sex-fully teach you Latin;
The root of all words…
As you cum translate my vernacular….

Ssshhhh…
Do not disturb me during my fantasies…
Just take full accountability for the passion
Which you evoke inside of me
And my circadian inebriated
Evening day dreams of being close to you…

Lustfully hug me again…
Tighter… Take the wheel sweetheart
I AM intoxicated by your lingering cologne
Sext me a citation… ordinance 69 code 2013…
…then dial 911 and call the doctors' office…
Forewarn the BR not ER that I'm Cumming…

I'm going to magnanimously die smiling
Right In the middle of a cheerful cardiac arrest …
I've been loving you under the influence recklessly
…. And I like it… Don't Stop!

Jamie Bond from UnMuted ink

Leather & Lace Rated S&M Sensual and Mature
http://tiny.cc/9xo1gx

Hot Summer Nights 2014

The Words Wouldn't Come

It was clearly a dream.
I am still breathing.
My head shook from side to side.
Twisted pearl earrings,
encased in knotted hair
found in the morning light.

The veins pumped hard as a
chill slithered down my neck.
It crawled across my shoulder,
and traced my clavicle. My
nipples were easily taut.

My body started to ache and quake.
Like the urgency of a drowning man,
I was gurgling and gasping for air,
then I tried to speak.

I looked over and there lie a
man; blissfully unaware
right next to me.
Still the words wouldn't come.

With the sweat now trickling
I realized that I was passing
into another form of life.
Self pleasure while sleeping
deep in this wet ardent state.

Janet Caldwell
http://www.janetcaldwell.com

inseparable

we were as supple as honeysuckle
as i suckled upon her every appendage
and her nipple hardened breast

our bodies were entwined
like that vive
growing upon the trellis

she was as sweet as the most delectable grape
yielding unto me
her early Spring Wine
and i was deeply intoxicated
by her very essence,
the taste of her

we both were insatiable

we were good together
she gave, i took
i inhaled, she sighed,
she moaned, i kissed her
deeply

yes she was my Yin
and i was her Yang,
we were inseparable

as the Ocean of sweat puddled
upon the Satin sheets beneath us
i understood
that we were not dividing our firmaments
like God did,
but we were bringing them together

Hot Summer Nights 2014

we were forcing a conjugal oneness
that will prevail
for all of eternity

our hips met
at the fork in the road
and we took the same path
seeking a higher understanding
of our ecstasy
and our bliss
as we kissed
each other

her lips were as giving
as her body
and my own
we were immersed
in an saliva-tory offering

our tongues were dancing
in that ring of fire
as our passions increased
and consumed
not only us
mentally
spiritually
emotionally
lustfully
as our loins
met on this hallowed ground

we were the universe
bursting with Supernovas of heat
creating and exploring
new galaxies of wonder

spawning new life
with exponential possibilities
of a new Utopia

and i saw the light

there was a very subtle yet frantic-ness
to our movements
we were smooth
like a well oiled machine

she gave me the lubrication
i needed
and i used it
for our movements had purpose

the moist heat
of our union
had a scent,
a taste that wafted in the air
a instinctual wantonness
and our hunger for each other
could not be abated

at times
we were in sync
and at times angry
for we could not get enough
of each other
and our hips attacked
as if this was our only chance
to cum together

Hot Summer Nights 2014

she opened,
i explored
she offered unto me
her Volcanic Womb
and i gave her my Lava
and she wrapped her legs around me
so that i could not escape,
but who wanted to ?
this was orgasmic

she was my shadow of love
and i was hers
she was my sunshine
and i was her light
and yes
we were inseparable

'just bill'

© 6 June 2014 : william s. peters, sr.

www.iamjustbill.com

i want you

i want to taste your heaven
i want your sweet soft succulent thighs
to part for me
as your eyes for me
beg me
beg me for more of me

i will delicately
peel back the folds
of your womanhood
that i may soon come to taste
your delectable delicacies
with my own certainty
of tongue

it's educated

your little girl in the boat
awaits my presence
as she stands aroused
beckoning me to find her
that i may adorn her
with my kisses of adoration
and nibble delicately
as you squiggle and wiggle
for more

i will lather her
and bathe her
with my wantonness for you
that which i have dreamed of
more times than i care to remember

Hot Summer Nights 2014

Eryka said
"Maybe Next Lifetime"
but i do not have the time
to put aside
that which can be made manifest
this day
today
right NOW !!!

as my tongue caresses your inner thighs
i look back into those eyes
of yours
and i see that you are lost
but know that i have come to save you
and you will cum for me
before i cum in you
that too
is certain

the curtains have been drawn
and it is time for the play
to begin
lights, camera, action
for this is no work for me
as i begin to get my work for you
in

sin, fuck that
this shit is good
and my wood
salutes and confirms this
this bliss i am now indulging in

i imagine you in kind
as you kindly

return my favor
as i savor this elixir
of your passions

you take me,
my manhood
and you touch me
in a way
only you can
and man am i beginning
to lose my self
as well

i am starting to swell
with a need for you
and you know this
as you have always known
i have seeds to be sown

you take me
in between your lips
as my hips
rise to greet you
and you smile
for you are my Mistress
of my pleasure
for you know where my treasure lies . . .
in you

you lock those lips softly
under the ridge of my helmet
and teasingly tease
despite my pleas
for more

Hot Summer Nights 2014

in the mean time
with my mouth wide open
and you sitting upon my face
there is little space
for my breath
so i eat
and i eat
while plunging my tongue
deep

the sound of sloppiness
fills the room
as i try my best
to stick this tongue
in your womb
and you assist me
without resisting me
as you grind down harder
as you now take me deeper
into my own erogenous imaginings
which have finally
become true

yes you
yes you

i want you

we only just begun . . . (Song)

'just bill'

www.iamjustbill.com

yes . . . i want

i want to whisper sweet things into your ear until they start to drip with honey and i want to watch as the sugar slowly crystallizes so i can suck on your lobes forever . . .ya ready ? . . . do you hear me ?

i want to visit your Holy Garden and plant deep kisses in your furrow that i may restructure your mind and your vocabulary so that the only three words you will ever utter again in your life are "Oh Bill mmmmmmmmmmm"

i want to lick your Desires of Divine Ecstasy until you want no more, for that is what i have come for, to make you my Vision, my Blissful Objective and i your Dream Master.

i want you to scream those three words i have taught you every time you blink your eyes for i am all you see . . . me, preparing you once again for that next step as you taste of this heaven where we become eternally fused and connected in the Communion of a Love that makes the Angels blush and God smile.

i want to teach you the Acrobatics of Love beyond understandings of possibilities, i want to teach you those positions that make the Kama Sutra blush deeply and run away and hide like the Kids Play it is.

Hot Summer Nights 2014

i want you to hold my Head Softly, Delicately, Lovingly upon your Nipple Hardened Breast, where i rest in between every Breath and every Heartbeat, for you complete me as i complete you, for i am your life essence as you are mine.

i want to kneel before your Holy Fountain of Love and drink the warm liquid of your passions until i am filled with the Spirit of an Orgasmic Joy and Sweetness that was meant only for me . . . a place where i become the Universe and my eyes twinkle brighter than the Stars of all the Heavens created and those yet to come . . . i want to taste your Rainbows . . . let me be that one and only one who can drink from that Sacred place of thy Divine Essence and Beauty . . .

i want you to dance for me in your Dreams . . . in your Reality in your every cell . . every pore . . . every thought . . . listen to the music that is coming to you as i am coming for you . . . let us dance with a fervor that manifests our expectations into possibilities and thus into our reality . . let us loose our selves this day, this moment in the eternity of the happiness we were borne to experience .. . i want you to dance that dance upon my loins that urges me to release this liquid fire in your womb that we can birth a new truth to the Garden of Life that all may Drink, all may taste our Truth of what Love and Passion is . . let us dance the dance of smiles and finally . . .

i want you to be thankful for every wrong turn you have made upon the Road of life for it was those wrong turns that were the right turns, for they brought you to me, for i have been waiting for you a Lifetime . . . and the song of your heart you now sing makes Flowers Dance and Butterflies Smile and God pats Himself on the back as He says to Himself "Well Done"

yes . . . i want . . . You . . . what do you want ?

'just bill'

www.iamjustbill.com

Hot Summer Nights 2014

is it time for a Cold Shower yet ?

epilogue

www.inerchildpress.com

other Anthologies

Check out all of our Anthologies

http://www.innerchildpress.com/anthologies-sales-special.php

If you are a Writer, Poet and are looking to be published . . .
stop by and check us out . . .

www.innerchildpress.com

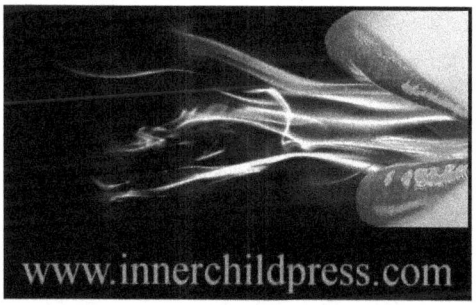

let us celebrate our Magic with you !

Other Anthologies by Inner Child Press

Other Anthologies by Inner Child Press

Other Anthologies by Inner Child Press

Other Anthologies by Inner Child Press

A GATHERING OF WORDS

POETRY & COMMENTARY
FOR
TRAYVON MARTIN

Other Anthologies by Inner Child Press

Other Anthologies by Inner Child Press

Mandela

The Man

His Life

Its Meaning

Our Words

Poetry ... Commentary & Stories
The Anthological Writers

Other Anthologies by Inner Child Press

a collection of the Voices of Many inspired by ...

Monte Smith

Other Anthologies by Inner Child Press

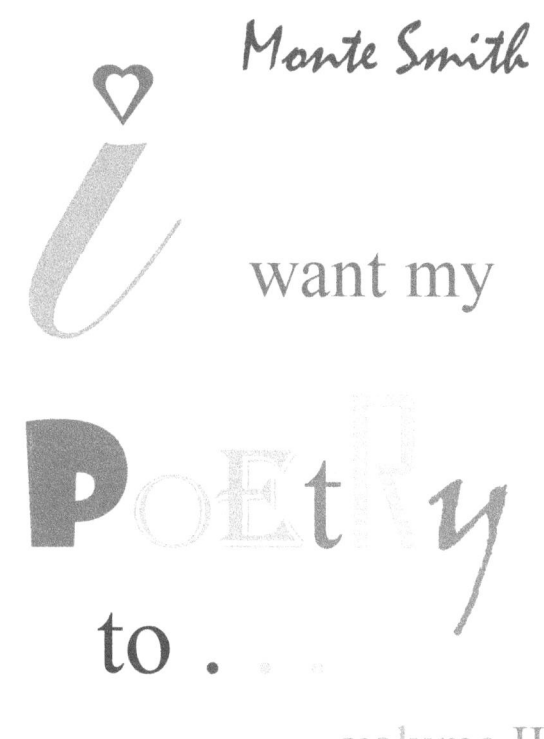

a collection of the Voices of Many inspired by . . .

Monte Smith

i want my PoEtRy to . . .

volume II

Other Anthologies by Inner Child Press

11 Words

|||| ||||

(9 lines . . .)

for those who are challenged

an anthology of Poetry inspired by . . .

Poetry Dancer

Other Anthologies by Inner Child Press

Other Anthologies by Inner Child Press

Other Anthologies by Inner Child Press

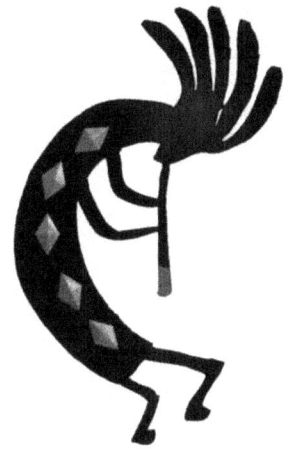

a
Poetically
Spoken
Anthology
volume I
Standard Edition

Other Anthologies by Inner Child Press

a
Poetically
Spoken
Anthology
volume I
Collector's Edition

Other Anthologies by Inner Child Press

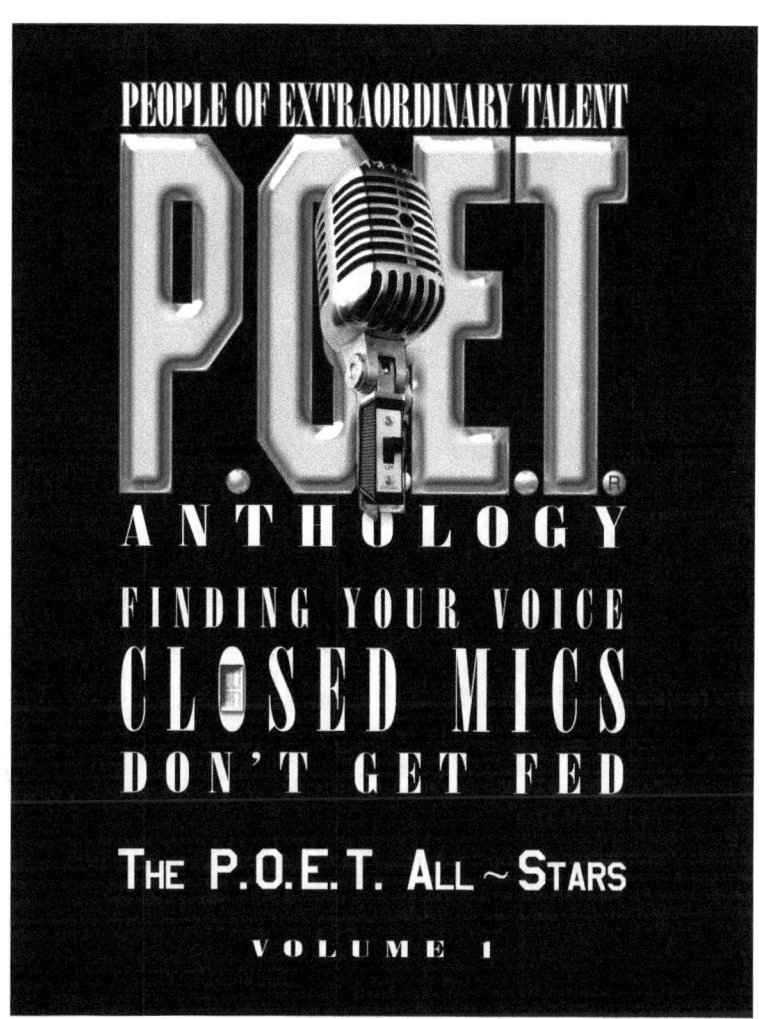

Other Anthologies by Inner Child Press

Other Anthologies by Inner Child Press

www.worldhealingworldpeacepoetry.com

Other Anthologies by Inner Child Press

www.worldhealingworldpeacepoetry.com

Other Anthologies by Inner Child Press

www.worldhealingworldpeacepoetry.com

Other Anthologies by Inner Child Press

www.worldhealingworldpeacepoetry.com

Other Anthologies by Inner Child Press

The Year of the Poet
January 2014

The Poetry Posse

Jamie Bond
Gail Weston Shazor
Albert 'Infinite' Carrasco
Siddartha Beth Pierce
Janet P. Caldwell
June 'Bugg' Barefield
Debbie M. Allen
Tony Henninger
Joe DaVerbal Minddancer
Robert Gibbons
Neetu Wali
Shareef Abdur-Rasheed
William S. Peters, Sr.

Carnation

Our January Feature
Terri L. Johnson

Free Download

http://www.innerchildpress.com/the-year-of-the-poet

Other Anthologies by Inner Child Press

the Year of the Poet

February 2014

violets

The Poetry Posse

Jamie Bond
Gail Weston Shazor
Albert 'Infinite' Carrasco
Siddartha Beth Pierce
Janet P. Caldwell
June 'Bugg' Barefield
Debbie M. Allen
Tony Henninger
Joe DaVerbal Minddancer
Robert Gibbons
Neetu Wali
Shareef Abdur-Rasheed
William S. Peters, Sr.

Our February Features
Teresa E. Gallion & Robert Gibson

Free Download

http://www.innerchildpress.com/the-year-of-the-poet

Other Anthologies by Inner Child Press

Free Download

http://www.innerchildpress.com/the-year-of-the-poet

Other Anthologies by Inner Child Press

the Year of the Poet

April 2014

The Poetry Posse

Jamie Bond
Gail Weston Shazor
Albert 'Infinite' Carrasco
Siddartha Beth Pierce
Janet P. Caldwell
June 'Bugg' Barefield
Debbie M. Allen
Tony Henninger
Joe DaVerbal Minddancer
Robert Gibbons
Neetu Wali
Shareef Abdur-Rasheed
Kimberly Burnham
William S. Peters, Sr.

Our April Featured Poets

Fahredin Shehu
Martina Reisz Newberry
Justin Blackburn
Monte Smith

Sweet Pea

celebrating international poetry month

Free Download

http://www.innerchildpress.com/the-year-of-the-poet

Other Anthologies by Inner Child Press

the year of the poet
May 2014

May's Featured Poets

ReeCee
Joski the Poet
Shannon Stanton

Dedicated To our Children

The Poetry Posse

Jamie Bond
Gail Weston Shazor
Albert 'Infinite' Carrasco
Siddartha Beth Pierce
Janet P. Caldwell
June 'Bugg' Barefield
Debbie M. Allen
Tony Henninger
Joe DaVerbal Minddancer
Robert Gibbons
Neetu Wali
Shareef Abdur-Rasheed
Kimberly Burnham
William S. Peters, Sr.

Lily of the Valley

Free Download

http://www.innerchildpress.com/the-year-of-the-poet

Other Anthologies by Inner Child Press

the Year of the Poet
June 2014

Love & Relationship

Rose

June's Featured Poets
Shantelle McLin
Jacqueline D. E. Kennedy
Abraham N. Benjamin

The Poetry Posse
Jamie Bond
Gail Weston Shazor
Albert 'Infinite' Carrasco
Siddartha Beth Pierce
Janet P. Caldwell
June 'Bugg' Barefield
Debbie M. Allen
Tony Henninger
Joe DaVerbal Minddancer
Robert Gibbons
Neetu Wali
Shareef Abdur-Rasheed
Kimberly Burnham
William S. Peters, Sr.

Free Download

http://www.innerchildpress.com/the-year-of-the-poet

This Anthological Publication
is underwritten solely by

Inner Child Press

Inner Child Press is a Publishing Company Founded and Operated by Writers. Our personal publishing experiences provides us an intimate understanding of the sometimes daunting challenges Writers, New and Seasoned may face in the Business of Publishing and Marketing their Creative "Written Work".

For more Information

Inner Child Press

www.innerchildpress.com

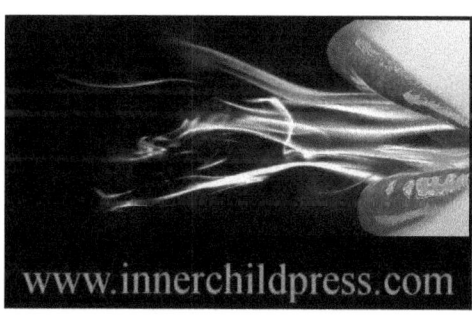

www.ingramcontent.com/pod-product-compliance
Lightning Source LLC
Chambersburg PA
CBHW070801100426
42742CB00012B/2212